THE ABCs OF A FIRST LADY

I have something to say!

Pastor Jacqueline Renee Duncan

The ABCs Of A First Lady
"I Have Something to Say!"

Published by
Kingdom Publishing, LLC
1350 Blair Drive, Ste F
Odenton, MD 21113

Printed in the United States of America

ISBN: 978-1-967006-28-1 (Paperback)

Unless otherwise noted, all scripture quotations are from the King James Version of the Holy Bible (KJV), public domain. Scriptures marked NIV are taken from the NEW INTERNATIONAL VERSION (NIV): Scripture taken from THE HOLY BIBLE, NEW INTERNATIONAL VERSION®. Copyright©1973, 1978, 1984, 2011 by Biblica, Inc.™. Used by permission of Zondervan. Scriptures marked TLB are taken from the THE LIVING BIBLE (TLB): Scripture taken from THE LIVING BIBLE copyright© 1971. Used by permission of Tyndale House Publishers, Inc., Carol Stream, Illinois 60188. All rights reserved. Scriptures marked ESV are taken from the THE HOLY BIBLE, ENGLISH STANDARD VERSION (ESV): Scriptures taken from THE HOLY BIBLE, ENGLISH STANDARD VERSION ® Copyright© 2001 by Crossway, a publishing ministry of Good News Publishers. Used by permission. Scriptures marked NKJV are taken from the NEW KING JAMES VERSION (NKJV): Scripture taken from the NEW KING JAMES VERSION®. Copyright© 1982 by Thomas Nelson, Inc. Used by permission. All rights reserved. Scriptures marked AMP are taken from the AMPLIFIED BIBLE (AMP): Scripture taken from the AMPLIFIED® BIBLE, Copyright © 1954, 1958, 1962, 1964, 1965, 1987 by the Lockman Foundation Used by Permission. (www.Lockman.org). Scripture quotations marked TPT are from The Passion Translation®. Copyright © 2017, 2018, 2020 by Passion & Fire Ministries, Inc. Used by permission. All rights reserved. ThePassionTranslation.com.

Table of Contents

Introduction

by Pastor Jacqueline Renee Duncan

In the heart of nearly every church stands a woman whose presence is both visible and invisible at the same time. She is seen standing beside the pastor, greeting the congregation, supporting the ministry, encouraging the women, praying with the hurting, and carrying herself with dignity and grace. Yet much of what she carries cannot be seen.

She is the First Lady.

Her role is not one that is chosen by election or earned through an application. It is not a position that comes with a handbook or a clearly defined job description. Instead, it is a sacred assignment that unfolds over time — often quietly, sometimes painfully, but always purposefully.

The title "First Lady" may be given by the church, but the calling behind it is given by God.

To be a pastor's wife is to stand in a unique intersection of ministry, marriage, and mission. It is a life lived in public while carrying many private burdens. It is a calling that requires strength, patience, wisdom, discernment, and above all, a deep and abiding relationship with God.

Many people see the platform, but they do not see the preparation.

They see the smile on Sunday morning but may never see the late-night prayers. They hear the encouraging words but may not realize the emotional weight that comes with loving people through their pain, disappointments, and struggles.

The life of a First Lady is often filled with beautiful moments of ministry — but it is also marked by seasons of growth, stretching, and sacrifice.

This book, The ABC's of a First Lady, was created to speak honestly and encouragingly into that journey.

Rather than presenting a rigid formula for how a First Lady should serve, this book invites you into a collection of voices and experiences from women who have walked this road. Each chapter reflects the wisdom, challenges, victories, and lessons learned along the way.

From A for Apprehended by God to Z for Zeal While You Heal, every letter represents a different dimension of the calling.

Each chapter is written from the heart of women who understand what it means to walk this path — women who have prayed through difficult nights, navigated complex relationships, supported their husbands through the pressures of leadership, and still found joy in serving God's people.

These pages are not meant to create unrealistic expectations. Instead, they are meant to remind you that you are not alone.

Introduction

For some readers, this book may affirm what you have already experienced. You may find yourself nodding as you read, recognizing the familiar challenges and blessings that come with this calling.

For others, this book may serve as preparation for seasons you have not yet encountered. It may offer perspective and encouragement as you grow into the fullness of the role God has entrusted to you.

And for those who may be feeling weary or discouraged, these pages are meant to remind you that the God who called you is faithful to sustain you.

Being a First Lady does not mean having all the answers. It does not mean never experiencing moments of doubt or fatigue. It does not require perfection.

What it does require is faithfulness.

Faithfulness to God.

Faithfulness to your marriage.

Faithfulness to the people you serve.

Faithfulness to the unique calling God has placed on your life.

One of the greatest misconceptions about the role of a First Lady is that she must fit into a particular mold — that she must dress a certain way, speak a certain way, or serve in a particular ministry capacity.

But God does not call women to copy one another.

He calls them to be authentic.

Some First Ladies are teachers.

Some are intercessors.

Some are organizers.

Some are counselors.

Some are worship leaders.

Some serve quietly behind the scenes.

The diversity of gifts among pastors' wives is not a weakness in the church — it is a reflection of the creativity of God.

The purpose of this book is not to define what a First Lady must be, but to affirm what she already is:

A woman chosen by God for a unique assignment.

Throughout these chapters you will encounter stories of perseverance, vulnerability, growth, healing, leadership, and faith. You will see how God shapes His daughters through the joys and the challenges of ministry life.

You will also discover that while the role of a First Lady may carry many expectations from people, the most important expectation comes from God — to walk faithfully with Him.

When a woman learns to root her identity not in the opinions of others but in the presence of God, she finds the strength to serve with freedom rather than pressure.

She discovers that her value does not come from a title but from her relationship with Christ.

And when that truth settles in the heart, ministry becomes less about performance and more about purpose.

As you begin this journey through the alphabet of calling, allow yourself the grace to reflect, to learn, and to grow.

Take time to consider the experiences shared by these women and the lessons that resonate with your own story.

You may laugh.

You may feel encouraged.

You may even recognize parts of your own journey reflected in these pages.

But above all, my prayer is that you will be reminded of something essential:

God saw you before anyone else called you "First Lady."

He knew the path you would walk.

He knew the people you would serve.

And He knew the strength He would place inside of you.

So as you turn these pages, open your heart, reflect on your own journey, and allow God to speak to you through the voices of women who understand the beauty and the burden of this calling.

Welcome to The ABC's of a First Lady.

Apprehended: Chosen, Captured, and Called to the Front Lines

By Dr. Barbara A. Palmer

"Not that I have already obtained all this, or have already been made perfect, but I press on to take hold of that for which Christ Jesus took hold of me." — Philippians 3:12 (NIV)

When I think about the word apprehended, it takes me back to the Apostle Paul's deeply personal reflection in Philippians 3. In just a few lines, Paul gives voice to something that many of us as pastors' wives have felt but may have never put into words: "I haven't arrived. I haven't figured it all out. But Christ got a hold of me—and now I'm living to get a hold of what got a hold of me."

That, my sister, is what it means to be apprehended. You didn't just say "yes" to a man—you said "yes" to a mantle. You didn't just fall in love with someone who preaches—you fell into the hands of a holy assignment, one that would stretch you, shape you, and sometimes shake you to your core. But here's the truth that anchors me even when the assignment feels heavy: You were apprehended for this.

Apprehended Means Chosen With Intention

Paul didn't stumble into ministry—he was stopped, arrested, and apprehended on the road to Damascus. It wasn't gentle or gradual; it was a divine interruption. The same is true for many of us. God interrupted our plans, our comfort zones, and even our identities to usher us into a role that we didn't necessarily apply for—but were appointed to.

I remember when I first stepped into the role of "First Lady." It didn't come with a manual. There was no initiation ceremony—just a whirlwind of expectations, assumptions, and silent pressures. People saw the title and the heels. They didn't see the tears behind closed doors. But even in the confusion, I heard God whisper, *You've been apprehended. I chose you with intention. This is not random. This is divine.*

Apprehension isn't about being trapped—it's about being trusted. God saw something in you before you ever saw it in yourself. He knew that your presence would calm storms, that your prayers would break chains, and that your voice would carry healing—even if it trembled while speaking.

Apprehended Means Surrendered to Purpose

Being apprehended doesn't just mean being chosen. It means being yielded. It means realizing you don't belong to yourself anymore. Your steps, your words, your posture—even your silence—are vessels through which God moves.

There are days I've wanted to run. Days when I've questioned whether I'm cut out for this. Days I've cried in the bathroom after church because someone criticized the way I worship, dress, or parent. But then I remember: Apprehended women don't run from the call—we run toward the Cross.

Paul said he was pressing toward what Christ had already apprehended him for. That means the purpose is already inside of you. You're not chasing destiny—you're growing into it. There is a reason you're the one He chose to walk alongside that man of God. There's a reason you're planted in that church, in that season, with those people. It's because your surrender carries power.

Apprehended Means Covered and Kept

One of the most beautiful revelations of being apprehended is this: You are not alone. To be apprehended by God is to be held by Him. I know it may not always feel that way—especially when you're carrying everyone's burdens, managing your own household, raising children, and still showing up to lead worship, host women's gatherings, or pray over the sick.

But you are not forgotten in the crowd. God didn't just call your husband—He captured you, too. And what God captures, He keeps. What He keeps, He covers.

There have been moments when I've said, "Lord, I'm tired of being strong." And in those moments, I felt the Spirit remind me, "I'm strong in you. Rest in My grip. You've been apprehended—and I'm not letting go."

The Weight of the Mantle—and the Grace to Carry It

Let's be real. Being a pastor's wife can feel like spiritual whiplash. One day you're celebrated; the next, you're criticized. You're expected to be visible but not flashy, humble but not invisible, supportive but not too opinionated. It's like walking a tightrope blindfolded—with people shouting directions from every side.

But here's what I've learned: the weight of the mantle comes with the grace to carry it. You are not just a supporting character in your husband's story. You're a leading lady in God's narrative of redemption. You hold keys in the Spirit. You are a thermostat in your church. You shape the culture without ever taking the mic.

And when your knees hit the floor in prayer, all of heaven pays attention—because you've been apprehended.

What Does It Look Like to Live Apprehended?

Let me give you some signs that you're walking in your divine apprehension:

1. You feel stretched beyond comfort.
2. You have a burden you didn't choose.
3. You keep showing up.
4. You have private battles with public consequences.

Apprehended but Not Abandoned

You may feel misunderstood. You may feel like you're living in a glass house. You may even feel like no one checks on you unless they need you. But hear me clearly: You are not abandoned. You are not forgotten.

God is near to every sigh, every sacrifice, and every seed you've sown in secret. He will reward your faithfulness. He will strengthen your heart. And He will continue to reveal the reason why He apprehended you in the first place.

To My Fellow Pastor's Wife...

You are not just "the First Lady." You are a forerunner.

You are not just "the Pastor's Wife." You are a pillar.

You are not just supporting the ministry. You are a strategic part of God's plan to advance His Kingdom.

Let your yes be full. Let your pressing be intentional. Let your tears be sacred. Because you were apprehended on purpose, for a purpose.

A Final Word from Paul... and From Me

Paul said, "I press on." Why? Because he knew the One who called him wasn't finished with him yet. And neither is He finished with you.

So press on, woman of God.

Press on through the criticism.

Press on through the spiritual warfare.

Press on through the loneliness.

Press on—because you were apprehended for such a time as this.

A Prayer for the Apprehended Wife

Father, thank You for apprehending me with purpose. Thank You for trusting me with this mantle, even when I feel overwhelmed by the weight of it. Remind me daily that I was chosen with intention, captured with love, and called with divine authority. Strengthen my hands when they grow weak. Restore my heart when it feels weary. Let me never forget that I am held by You. I surrender to the purpose for which You took hold of me. In Jesus' name, Amen.

About the Author

Dr. Barbara Palmer is a visionary leader, author, speaker, and transformational coach with more than 30 years of experience serving children, youth, families, and faith communities.

She is the Founder and CEO of Kingdom Kare, Inc., a nonprofit organization dedicated to providing personalized care, educational programs, mentorship, and community support that empower individuals to pursue and achieve their dreams.

Through Kingdom Kare, Dr. Palmer has developed impactful programs including early childhood education, a family support center for teen mothers, violence interruption initiatives, mentoring programs, food distribution, and community health outreach. Her work has helped transform countless lives while building stronger communities.

Dr. Palmer is also the co-founder and apostolic leader of Kingdom Celebration Center alongside her husband, Apostle Antonio Palmer, where she trains leaders, ministers, and intercessors while equipping believers to walk boldly in their calling.

An accomplished author of multiple books, Dr. Palmer is passionate about leadership development, faith-driven entrepreneurship, and empowering women to transform their lives spiritually, personally, and professionally. Her voice carries both wisdom and authenticity as she teaches others how to lead with purpose while creating lasting impact.

Dr. Palmer continues to inspire audiences across the nation through mentoring, consulting, writing, and ministry.

Bold Faith

By Pastor Shawn Moss

Experiencing the bold side of faith changes everything. There is a recharge of faith that makes you radical, unshakable, and bold—defying the odds. It will make you speak life where death seems to be the only thing you see in the natural. Bold faith takes you beyond the world we live in by unraveling logical thinking and natural beliefs. It taps into the spiritual core of faith. If you have not noticed, this natural world has fading values, and the truth of God is under attack on every side. Bold faith makes you see through the eyes of faith—victory over every attack and the manifestation of the promises of God.

Come with me on the path of faith. With each step, release yourself to make your footsteps louder, stronger, and bolder. Let's deal with bold faith—the kind of faith that is audacious and unshakable even when it seems like everything around you is faithless. Understanding what this kind of faith looks like for your personal walk, your family, your body, and more is important. Walk through this chapter and allow God's voice to arise above life's noise as your faith becomes bolder.

Imagine faith as a long suspension bridge that stretches across a huge canyon. On one side is everything you've prayed for—your healing, breakthrough, restoration, and increase. On the other side is where you are now. That place you currently stand in could be a place of hurt, of waiting, or of trusting. As you look across to the other side, your natural eye sees the bridge swaying from side to side. It hears the howls of the wind. Then you step out, but soon realize that each step requires trust as you continue to move forward. Bold faith requires motion. You can't stay in one place; it moves you to the next step. Even when others refuse to take a step, you must stay in motion.

Hebrews 11:1 reminds us,

"Now faith is the substance of things hoped for, the evidence of things not seen." (KJV)

Faith doesn't deny reality—it defies it, because the greater truth is that God's report is victory. I understand what the report says, but I know what God said. Bold faith does not move according to what the circumstance looks like, but according to who God is.

There are many places in your life where bold faith can reside. I believe that a great area to activate bold faith first is in our homes. The enemy knows if he can break up the family, he can fracture the future. We know fractures heal in time, but we also know they can be prevented. So we are called to intercede and intercept for our families, not retreat. It is imperative to do it as boldly as Joshua in the Bible, declaring, "But as for me and my house, we will serve the Lord." (Joshua 24:15 KJV)

Joshua declared this in the midst of the people of Israel being surrounded by idol worship, divided loyalty, and forgetfulness of God's goodness.

Nevertheless, Joshua rose up and drew a line in the sand as a bold father, a faith-filled man who dared to believe God. Reading this is your sign to believe God. Don't lose faith, but increase faith and believe boldly. The world may say that when you get to a certain point it is beyond repair. It may even say that when you get to a certain point in health there is no repair.

Allow your bold faith to declare: You are not forsaken. Your family is not broken. Prayers are not forgotten. God is able!

Faith for your family means believing that God's promises are greater than their current path or circumstance. Begin to pray and speak life even when things look dead. Have faith that refuses to agree with what you see in the natural. Instead, choose to see resurrection in everything that aligns with the promises and will of God.

Bold Faith in Healing

Sometimes the greatest test of faith comes when the diagnosis arrives and the attack is in our own bodies or in that of a loved one. The test magnifies when the pain doesn't stop, when the symptoms remain, and when the doctors continue to give the same report. But understand this—your body is still under the covenant of healing. Jesus completed the finished work on the cross. Jesus didn't just die for your salvation; He died for your wholeness. Therefore, healing is not being wishful—it is a blood-bought promise.

The woman in Mark 5 suffered with an issue of blood for twelve years. The doctors failed her, her money was gone, and her strength was depleted. The only thing left was faith. The truth is, even though her issue seemed impossible, she was still alive. She was alive enough to go after Jesus and touch the hem of His garment. It wasn't just her—her faith was alive. Tell your faith to wake up and come alive. When Jesus felt virtue leave Him, He said, "Daughter, thy faith hath made thee whole; go in peace…" (Mark 5:34, KJV)

I too had an issue. Almost seventeen years ago, my health took a sudden turn and began to fail. I had recently delivered our third child, and after a month of enjoying my smiling, joyful son, my body began to hurt. It was something I had never experienced in my life. My hands, arms, feet, and legs felt like needles and pins—tingling every hour of the day, even going numb at times. No matter what I did, it wouldn't go away. I can remember going to the emergency room one night, and after a series of tests, I was diagnosed with multiple sclerosis.

I heard the diagnosis, but my faith refused to accept it because it did not align with the blood-bought healing of Jesus Christ. This began a whirlwind of more tests and doctors' appointments. In the midst of it all, I continued to care for my family, serve my church, lead praise and worship every Sunday, attend rehearsals, and more. No one but my husband and sister knew that I was dealing with so much pain. I didn't even tell anyone about the diagnosis. My condition seemed to be getting worse.

As the months went by, I continued to refuse to accept the diagnosis and kept reminding myself that by the stripes of Jesus Christ I am healed. My faith was so strong that I refused to medicate the issue—that was just where my level of faith was. It was in this season that I really activated bold faith. Now let me be clear—I'm not saying that you should not take your medicine, because I understand that everyone may not be able to take their faith that far. But what I am saying is that this is what I did according to my faith. I reminded myself that I was healed, even with symptoms. It was a journey to get to a symptom-free, healed state.

In due time, I went to get an MRI and found out that the spots that were on my brain had disappeared. Multiple sclerosis was no longer there. My body had aligned with the finished work of Christ. Hallelujah!

Sometimes the manifestation of healing is automatic. It's instant. But sometimes it is a process. Either way, hold tight to bold faith and trust God. Declare confidently that you believe God in spite of the pain in your body. Believe God even when the doctor says otherwise. Believe Jehovah Rapha, your healer. Perhaps you're walking through sickness right now. Please know this: God is there. God sees you. God has not forgotten you. Healing is your portion.

What Bold Faith Looks Like

Bold faith stares fear eye to eye and tells it to go. It declares healed when pain is present. It speaks restoration over your child, even if they've spoken hate over you. It gives even when your bank account seems low. It continues to build even when others no longer believe. It isn't passive—it is as forceful as a blazing fire spreading to every corner of its surroundings. It stands in confidence, relentless in the storm. If you remember nothing else, remember this: Even if no one else believes—you believe God!

Speak this declaration of faith:

I declare today that my faith is firmly rooted in the promises of God, unshakable and fearless in the face of adversity. I will not shrink back. I will not be silent. I will not compromise the truth. I stand boldly, walking by faith and not by sight. I clothe myself in victorious strength, believing that mountains will move, doors will swing open, and miracles will manifest. I speak over my family, my body, my finances, my community, and my future. I reject all doubt and fear, and I receive the Spirit of power, love, and a sound mind. Today, I reignite faith and obedience over hesitation. My steps are steady, my faith is bold, and my victory is certain!

About the Author

Pastor Shawn Moss is a dynamic leader, speaker, and worshiper dedicated to strengthening faith, families, and communities. She serves as the Leading Lady of Point of Grace Church International in Metro Atlanta, where she ministers alongside her husband, Apostle Dr. R. D. Moss. An established worship leader and preacher in her own right, Pastor Moss is a sought-after conference speaker, recording artist, entrepreneur, and published author.

She is the founder of The BOLD Conference and the BOLD Movement, a growing initiative focused on building bold believers who live, lead, and serve with courage and conviction. Pastor Moss also serves as President of LSM Global Ministries and is the visionary behind The Point Center, a community organization designed to strengthen families and support community transformation.

With a professional background in media, Pastor Moss previously served as a radio news director and reporter. She holds a Bachelor of Arts in Mass Communications—Radio, Television, and Film from Clark Atlanta University and a Master of Public Administration from Kennesaw State University.

Above all, Pastor Moss loves God deeply and treasures her role as a devoted wife and the mother of six amazing children. Learn more at ladyshawnmoss.com or email ladyshawnmoss@yahoo.com.

Christ, the Center of My Joy

By Dr. Katrina Haskins

As I think of the goodness of Jesus Christ, I can't help but think of joy—unspeakable joy—and how His Word has been added to my life. The joy of the Lord is my strength. But before I learned about the Word, I knew the way my life was in 1995—a complete mess. It had to be someone greater on the inside, greater than me, and His name is Jesus the Christ, the solid rock on which I stand.

Oh yes, Jesus Christ visited me in a dream and said, "I am calling you as my minister." I thought, Say what? Um, You see my life. I was born in Rochester, New York, and raised in Washington, D.C., by my grandparents. As time went on, I began to rededicate my life back to God as a young girl who had gone to church but then backslid over the years. I moved to Texas in 1995, and this is where I heard the voice of God saying, "I am calling you out into ministry."

Christ is the center of my joy. After hearing the voice of God, I wanted more. I found a church home at that time, grew in the Word, and experienced the anointing of God's call on my life. I was not a pastor's wife at that time. I owned a beauty salon with no clients—OMG! Talking about Christ being the center of my joy—He asked me to volunteer at the nursing home doing the elderly's hair and reading the Bible to them. This taught me the Word and how to study.

I did not even have many clients coming to the beauty salon, but once I started obeying God's command to bless the elderly, visit the women's shelter, and also do jail ministry—teaching women all over Texas—that is when my business took off every week. I became fully aware of what being a servant is all about for the Kingdom of God. Talk about the joy this brought to my heart, knowing God did not forget about me or my personal needs. He is a rewarder of those who seek His way of doing things for the Kingdom.

After about two years, I met this wonderful, handsome young man who was a minister named Alan Haskins—known now as Bishop Haskins. We call him Doc Haskins, which God has honored us both with through Honorary Doctorates. He changed my life again for the better. We dated six months, have been married twenty-six years, and are loving it. And God spoke and said, "Start the church." OMG! Off to the races we went.

The first two years into our marriage, the Lord said, "I am calling the both of you to pastor in ministry together." He is the pastor, and I serve as the First Lady. We have been doing this for twenty-five years, to be exact, and we are still going strong as Word Alive Ministries in the city of Baytown, Texas. We have three adult children and six grands—our pride and joys.

My journey began twenty-five years ago as a First Lady, and I have experienced many ups and downs. Not having mentors at first was tough. I stayed in prayer, asking God to show me how to be the best First Lady I could be. But here I am now, with so many beautiful spiritual mentors. Dr. Jacqueline Duncan is one of the best of the best I know in real time today. Her support and love mean the world to my husband and me. There are many other spiritual leading ladies I adore, including my spiritual daughter, Lady Detreal Mathews—just a sweetheart—and I am glad to have them in my life. As First Lady, I had to totally trust God to get us through every step, and He did just that for years.

Later, I realized I needed help and guidance. Then I met other First Ladies who taught me some things—praise Jesus—and I am still a work in progress. I would not trade my position at all. I love being a pastor's wife—not all the drama that comes with it sometimes (LOL)—but it is a complete joy.

I have been lied on, talked about, abused, misused, and now I am a great woman of faith. Trials make us strong—praise God—and I will continue to fight the good fight of faith. The Bible says we will win (1 Timothy 6:12). My favorite scripture is Psalm 23. This concludes my article: "The Lord is my shepherd, and I shall not want."

God has blessed us over the years, and I am grateful. As First Lady, I am still on the battlefield and walking in the Word.

Pastors' wives often face loneliness, social isolation, and a lack of time with their families due to the demanding nature of ministry. They also struggle with immense pressure to be a certain way, the pain of church hurt, and balancing their own identity with the expectations of their role, which can lead to emotional exhaustion and a feeling of being constantly "on display." I can relate to this, but seeking God has allowed me to overcome so much of this. Now I have lots of support from other great leading First Ladies.

I have learned so many keys about being a pastor's wife. To share a few, the list includes:

Key Struggles

- **Loneliness and isolation:** They may find it difficult to form genuine, deep friendships within the church because people's motives can be suspect, or they may treat the relationship with the wife as a way to get closer to the pastor. This creates a sense of isolation, even when surrounded by people.

- **Lack of time:** The demands of ministry can mean the husband has little time for his wife and family. This can lead to disrupted plans, a feeling of competing with the church for his attention, and the frustration of having to explain why "Dad can't" join them.

- **Expectations and pressure:** There is often intense pressure to be a perfect example of faith, leading to feelings of insecurity and a fear of not being "worthy" or a "good enough" pastor's wife. They may feel they can't be vulnerable or show pain because they are expected to be strong.

- **Church hurt:** They are vulnerable to, and may be deeply hurt by, church members, leading to feelings of betrayal, criticism, and exhaustion that are often difficult to share with others.

- **Blurred identity:** It can be hard to maintain a personal identity separate from the role, as the church is often the center of their social life, family support, and sometimes financial support, putting all their "eggs in one basket."

- **Emotional exhaustion:** The combination of social pressure, family demands, and constant scrutiny can lead to emotional burnout and a need for a safe space to process these hardships.

Strategies for Overcoming Struggles

- **Prioritize personal well-being:** Set aside specific, protected time for family and for oneself to avoid ministry completely consuming life.

- **Seek outside support:** Build community and friendships outside of the church, and don't be afraid to seek professional counseling or guidance from a trusted mentor.

- **Manage expectations:** Recognize that people in the church are not always saintly, and be willing to let others be wrong about you. Focus on your relationship with God and let go of the need to control the opinions of others.

- **Communicate with your spouse:** Have open conversations with your husband about the challenges you are facing so you can work through them together.

- **Find a safe place for emotions:** Practice methods like soaking up love and encouragement when it happens and letting negativity bounce off like a rubber ball.

- **Remember who you are:** God has gifted you individually, and it is important to give yourself space to explore and fulfill those individual callings and joys outside of your husband's ministry.

Prayers that this will bless every pastor's wife! Speaking of prayer, the Word of God says, "Seek first the kingdom of God, and everything else will be added to you" (Matthew 6:33).

About the Author

Co-Pastor Dr. Katrina Haskins serves faithfully alongside her husband, Bishop Alan Haskins, as co-pastor of Word Alive Ministries in Baytown, Texas. She is a true example of the Proverbs 31 woman—a devoted servant of the Kingdom of God who has dedicated her life to teaching and sharing the gospel of Jesus Christ.

Dr. Haskins is a loving mother, grandmother, and a devoted wife of more than twenty-six years to Bishop Alan Haskins. Together, they have shepherded a ministry that extends beyond Baytown, Texas, impacting communities through outreach initiatives, conferences, and Christian education training. Their ministry is widely recognized for its commitment to serving others through food distribution programs, leadership development, and biblical teaching. In addition to her pastoral responsibilities, Dr. Haskins is an author, conference speaker, and educator who believes deeply in the power of words to transform lives. She oversees the Women's Ministry, where she passionately encourages women to understand their identity in Christ and walk confidently in their calling as daughters of God.

Dr. Haskins is committed to teaching women that they are more than conquerors and that they can become everything God has called them to be. When she is not serving in ministry, Co-Pastor Dr. Haskins enjoys reading, walking, relaxing, and spending time with her family and church family.

Distractions

By Lady Laura Simon

Dear pastor's wife, this was the chapter that almost wasn't. Girl, deliver me from the distractions. You know the ones—big ones, little ones, ugly ones, silly ones... alllll the ones. Because you know I had some. A plethora, if you will. As we know, anything we are attempting to do for Kingdom building and the women of God comes with distractions. Any thing that takes you off your game, diverts you from your purpose, or simply steers you in another direction is a distraction. This is not grammatically correct what I'm about to say, but I know you'll get it: just deliver me already. Get me away from all these d's of life so I can move forward.

When I think back to my younger pastor's wife days, I had a ton of d's. As a 28-year-old, newly pregnant and newly titled PW, I was full of doubt. I doubted my husband, his calling, my calling, the church, my pregnancy, and God. All these doubts led to discontent, disobedience, and the dashing of my dreams. I was unhappy because I felt I was way behind in starting a family. I got married late, so I was disappointed that my friends already had babies (plural), and I was pregnant with my first. I had been married for two years, and they had been married at least four years or more. Simply put, I just felt left behind and old. Old at 28. Breathe.

I was discontent because the church we—I mean, he (my husband Tony)—pastored was small. As in sixteen people… one person for each pew, and baby girl Kennedy in utero. Sigh. I was disgruntled and dismayed. Don't judge me. I came from a large Baptist church with a big ole building and a whole lot of people. And to make my discontent even worse, it was non-denominational. Drop the mic. At that time— cue the '90s (reminisce, lol)—that was not a plus. It was a minus. Enter discontent.

This was not my dream. This was not what I had envisioned nor planned. And because it wasn't what I wanted, dreamed, or planned, my not-so-sunny disposition opened me up to even more distractions. There were descriptions (labels) of what I should be, wear, have, and do. That was an aggravation and a distraction. Then there was my diet. Although I was pregnant, people were talking about my weight. Well, that's not entirely true. Mainly, I was talking about my weight. I've always had an issue with that particular "d" in my life, and now that I was with child, it became an obsession that would haunt me to this day. Dieting is a d-word that I am still wrestling with. More on that later.

There were decisions that had to be made and divisions among the people because the young Pastor-Husband wanted to take a traditional, non-denominational church in a new direction. That was another distraction because the people were disappointed at having to even look at change. Then there were discrepancies in the church's bookkeeping. Bring on the

D's! D for drama, discord, and dissension, which led to disobedience. And with that came all the delicious tea. The tea in the city was scorching hot! Dirty words and gossip coming from every direction.

I was so not prepared for the destruction of long-time friendships and fellowships over the explosive growth of our little church. We didn't know it yet, but our destiny was a dilemma for some and a threat—although not from our perspective—to many others. The outward display of displeasure at what was going on in our lives was disheartening, especially coming from so-called friends. That was a difficult season. I wish I knew then what I know now.

As a PW, it isn't wise to hold deeply disappointing thoughts inside. They can be quite destructive and dangerous. I believe those types of thoughts can cause PTSD. Sisters, I wouldn't be your friend if I didn't share something with you that I think will help you. Post-Traumatic Stress Disorder is real. Anxiety is real. Depression can be debilitating. Distress over the discovery of discrepancies in the character of supposedly good friends is real. B for betrayal—which can cause distress—is another distraction that will have you unhinged. It is okay not to be okay. Seek help. Jesus and therapy is an awesome blessing.

Did she say that out loud? Yes.

Deliver me from the fake and phony pastor's wife—the one who never goes through anything, but if she does, it's always "I'm fine," or "I'm good," or "I'm blessed," or "I don't want anybody in my business." Girl, please. He sees it. We see it. So you might as well say it.

Listen, full transparency here: a lot of days I get in my own way. I self-sabotage, doubt my abilities, and question myself and my decisions. I also have the tendency to overthink everything. Some days—quiet as it's kept—I even doubt God and some of His decisions and answers. That part.

You might be thinking, *Wow, she doubts God?* Yep. And let me tell you something else: sometimes my disobedience is disguised as an excuse, disguised as a valid reason to harbor anxiety and a wee bit of animosity toward the members about what they do and don't do. I find myself disregarding or downplaying my issues and almost giddily dwelling on theirs. After all, my issues—DBA sins—most definitely aren't as bad as theirs, right? Wrong.

Harboring those feelings creates a great big open door to the possibility of affecting your—my—our destiny.

"Confess your faults one to another, and pray one for another, that ye may be healed. The effectual fervent prayer of a righteous man availeth much." —James 5:16 (KJV)

So, I'm confessing. Sis, please pray that I be healed from these distractions.

Next—what are we to do with our current d's? Your current d's? The distractions. The many distractions. I'll go first and share mine, and you can see if any of yours are listed. Currently, I'm on a diet, in debt, and experiencing friend drama. I just got out of a dilemma but am doubtful about upcoming decisions concerning career and ministry. The discontent has dissipated, but the discrepancies in the character of supposed good friendships are really causing distress.

With that said, what words can I give you that will help in your whatever-season?

Cry out to God.

He's a Deliverer. You can trust Him. He never fails. And He is faithful.

How do I know? Because I'm an MWV—Ministry War Veteran. As an older, more seasoned pastor's wife (in year thirty-three), I definitely believe I'm finally equipped to share my honest thoughts about distractions. I say that because in the past I questioned my experience and doubted anyone wanted to hear what I had to say. But I do have something to say. Please hear me.

If you're a young PW, don't be like me.

If you're a seasoned veteran PW, don't be like me.

Be you.

Don't ask God to deliver you from your distractions; ask Him to help you *through* them. Let Him do the distracting from the distractions. His ways are better than your ways, and His plans are better than yours, too. His distractions are different. He can distract you with distractions that will help you and not harm you—push you, propel you, and lead you on the path toward your Big D: your dreams, your destiny.

So how do we get there?

First, dare to dream. That dream that's in your heart is from Him. Dare to ask for divine distractions and directions.

"…Then trust the Lord completely; don't ever trust yourself. In everything you do, put God first, and He will direct you and crown your efforts with success." —Proverbs 3:5–6 (TLB)

Next, take a chance. You won't fail—but if you do, so what? If it's a part that gets you to your destiny, then it's supposed to happen.

"And we know that all that happens to us is working for our good if we love God and are fitting into His plans." —Romans 8:28 (TLB)

Finally, trust that God has a plan for all your seasons. When you pray about your seasons—and all the distractions you will face—consult the Holy Spirit. Ask Him with an honest, open, and sincere heart. And be transparent; I can't stress that enough. He sees. There is nothing you can hide. He hears. He listens.

"For I know the plans I have for you, says the Lord. They are plans I have for good and not for evil, to give you a future and a hope. In those days when you pray, I will listen. You will find me when you seek me, if you look for me in earnest." Jeremiah 29:11-13 (TLB)

"Commit everything you do to the Lord. Trust Him to help you do it, and He will." Psalm 37:5 (TLB)

And that includes distractions.

About the Author

Lady Laura Simon Lady Laura Simon is a passionate speaker, teacher, and podcaster with a special heart for pastors' wives, millennials, and extraordinary women navigating the unique challenges of life and ministry. Known for her authenticity and transparency, she is dedicated to helping women live genuine, faith-filled lives—even when life in ministry feels like living in a fishbowl.

She is an award-winning, best-selling author and ministry leader who skillfully blends her educational background with her personal experiences as a pastor's wife. Through her writing, speaking, and mentoring, Laura offers practical wisdom and encouragement that helps women bridge the gap between faith and everyday life.

Laura and her husband, Pastor Tony Simon, lovingly serve together as the leaders of Covenant City Fellowship. After raising their four children—two daughters and two sons—they now embrace the season of being empty nesters while continuing their shared commitment to ministry and community. Lady Laura currently resides in California and continues to inspire women through her speaking engagements, podcast, and writing ministry.

You can connect with her at:

www.covenantcityfellowship.com
www.ladylaurasimon.com

EMBRACE
Embrace to Enter In and Enter In to Be Empowered!

By Lady Shearon Grant

It is imperative that we embrace what our Heavenly Father has ordained. Many pastors' wives grapple with the role and responsibility of being a pastor's wife. The truth is, we are only a pastor's wife because of our husbands. When we don't embrace who we are—and who we are married to—we are unintentionally rejecting a part of our marriage. This opens the door for strife, rejection, and division to set in.

I am a pastor's wife because my husband is a pastor. To be ashamed of this or to despise the position is a form of ungratefulness. We believe that God has chosen and appointed our husbands to lead and make a difference in this world. Therefore, it is a privilege that the Father has chosen us to represent Him and to help lead His people. It is an honor and should never be viewed as anything less.

Being a pastor's wife is not about other people—even though we are leading people. It's not primarily about the congregation. It's about what God wants to do through you. In Jeremiah 3:15, He says, "I will give you pastors according to my heart, which shall feed you with knowledge and understanding." So remember, we are His heart—a gift to the body of Christ, trusted by the Father to help His people grow spiritually. We must fully accept, hold close to our hearts, and walk in joy knowing who we represent.

So what do I mean when I say "embrace"? Just as you fully took on your husband's last name, our mindset should be that and even more when it comes to this position: fully accepting, fully supporting, and approaching the assignment with willingness, affection, and purpose. Matthew 19:6 says, "So they are no longer two, but one flesh. Therefore, what God has joined together, let no one put asunder." That includes you, Woman of God. We must endeavor to walk in unity, for it is good and pleasant when we walk as one (Psalm 133:1).

Our marriages grow stronger and more resilient to attacks from the enemy when we walk in agreement. Ecclesiastes 4:9–10 tells us, "Two are better than one, because they have a good reward for their labor: If either of them falls, one can help the other up. But pity anyone who falls and has no one to help them up." Together, we are better. Together, we can accomplish and overcome all things.

There's something powerful that happens when a husband and wife are on the same page. God shows up in a big way. When we're walking in unity, He blesses what we're doing. When we operate in agreement, God multiplies the fruit of our labor. This is the beauty of unity—it allows God's presence to dwell richly among us (Matthew 18:20). And where God is, there is always victory!

The ultimate goal is the Great Commission. So whatever gifts and skills God has given you are intended to help fulfill that mission. Truthfully, whether married or not, this is every believer's mission. As wives, we must understand how to take our desires, our dreams, and our goals and submit them to the overall plan of God for our husbands and families. Everything we do should complement and enhance the vision for the home, not compete with it.

We are not in competition with our husbands, and our callings are not less significant. God has established order—and in marriage, our husbands are the head. Submitting is not a dirty word; it simply means finding your proper relation to. How do I take what God has placed in me and build it with my husband? Be assured: what's inside of you is no surprise to God. He placed it there for a reason. And when we fully EMBRACE who our Heavenly Father has positioned us to be, then and only then can we ENTER IN.

Enter into what?

Remember, there is a life that God has already prepared for you. There are deep secrets He wants to reveal to you (1 Corinthians 2:9–10). The Lord desires to open His good treasure—the heavens—to you and your husband (Deuteronomy 28:12). He wants you to experience real joy, real peace, real love, real rest, and real prosperity. He has already given us access to it.

Woman of God, embrace this truth so you can enter into that realm. What realm, you ask? The realm where the Father's blessings dominate and prevail. The realm where your desires, dreams, and goals begin to manifest. The realm where you are living in green pastures (Psalm 23), enjoying perfect peace (Isaiah 26:3), and walking in divine rest—even while busy. The realm where ministry is no longer a chore, but a joy and a privilege.

Obedience is the key. Order is the way of the Kingdom. When we align ourselves with His will, everything flows more freely. Chaos is replaced with clarity. Frustration yields to fulfillment. Our obedience allows God to do what only He can—open doors no man can shut, soften hearts that seem immovable, and provide peace that surpasses all understanding.

When we trust Him, we experience His overflow.

Ephesians 3:20 says, "Now unto him that is able to do exceeding and abundantly above all that we ask or think, according to the power that worketh in us."

Embrace to Enter In and Enter In to Be Empowered.

Isn't it amazing that we have access to an all-powerful God—the One who created the heavens and the earth, the One who created this very day that you and I are living in, the One who knows our tomorrow?

Jesus said, "I have given you power to tread on serpents and scorpions and to overcome all the power of the enemy; nothing will harm you" (Luke 10:19). What a privilege to have access to His power—to be empowered to do great and mighty things in the name of Jesus! His power lives in us. It is not God's will that we struggle. Being a pastor's wife should be enjoyable because we understand the assignment.

If you dislike or even hate being a pastor's wife, then it is a sure sign you have the wrong view of what it means to be you. If you think wrong, you'll believe wrong. The wrong mindset causes us to carry burdens we were never meant to carry. Disliking this position often reveals a distorted view of God—and of marriage. At its core, this is a trust issue. Why would our Heavenly Father assign us to something that would destroy us? He wouldn't.

In closing, understand this: being an effective pastor's wife is directly tied to how we operate in our marriages. Our marriages must be aligned for the will of God to go forth in our homes, in our churches, and in the communities we serve. We are a team. We are powerful together. We can do more together than we ever could apart.

You might be saying, "That sounds great, and I want to embrace it—but someone needs to tell my husband! My husband doesn't think I should help lead the ministry. He says I'm too emotional, too sensitive, and should only focus on our home."

If this is you, don't be discouraged. It simply means you've got some work to do. And that's okay—growth is a journey. Start by spending more time with the Lord. Set aside time to worship, pray, study the Word, and listen for His voice. Know that while you're doing this, God is developing you spiritually. This isn't about your husband. It's not about gaining his approval to minister. This is for you.

Don't underestimate the power of your prayers or the influence you have with the Father and your husband. In due season, you will reap if you faint not (Galatians 6:9). Keep showing up in love.

We must be mature and spiritually developed before we can minister effectively to anyone—especially to those we are leading. I believe we can all agree with that.

As you begin to pray for yourself and for your husband, the Lord will begin to soften his heart and shift the atmosphere of your home. Proverbs 21:1 reminds us that "The king's heart is in the hand of the Lord, as the rivers of water: He turns it whithersoever He will."

Learning to embrace your role as a pastor's wife has nothing to do with a title. It's not about where you sit or what you wear. It's not about whether you preach or teach like your husband—or like anyone else. It's not about how many scriptures you can quote. It's not about how many people in your church like you (let's assume they all love you!). It's not about how big or small your ministry is.

It has everything to do with embracing who God called you to be. Embrace to Enter In and Enter In to Be Empowered!

About the Author

Lady Shearon Grant, affectionately known as *Lady Grant,* is a devoted wife, mother, and servant of God with a deep passion for empowering others through prayer, healing, and spiritual leadership. Her heart for ministry is especially evident in her dedication to encouraging and strengthening pastors' wives.

For more than a decade, Lady Grant has ministered to hundreds of pastors' wives through the Southeast Regional PW's Ministry, where women were inspired and equipped to Connect, Bond, Grow, and Serve in their unique callings alongside their spouses in ministry.

She faithfully serves alongside her husband, Pastor Jassen R. Grant, at Conquerors Church International in Kannapolis, North Carolina. Together, they have been blessed with three beautiful children and share decades of ministry experience.

Lady Grant continues to impact and uplift women through her monthly *Sisterhood Check-In* gatherings, where she creates safe spaces for encouragement, fellowship, and spiritual growth.

The Journey of the Favored

By Lady Althea Faye Bell

To be favored is to be chosen, distinguished, and graced with something extraordinary that sets you apart—not because life is easy, but because there is a divine purpose at work. I am First Lady Althea Faye Bell, and I am a living testament to what it means to be favored by God. My life's journey is more than a list of accomplishments or moments of resilience; it is the unfolding story of a woman walking under an open heaven, marked by grace, refined through fire, and called to make an impact. My name echoes not just in ministry, but in leadership, empowerment, and a life anchored in faith. Through every trial and triumph, through seasons of heartbreak and moments on the mountaintop, I remain undeniably and unapologetically FAVORED.

With a Purpose from Birth

From an early age, it was clear that I was different. Born into a family rich in love, legacy, and tradition, my spirit carried something unique even as a child. My wisdom often surpassed my years, and my deep love for faith and family laid the foundation for the woman I was destined to become. I was the kind of child who spoke life into the atmosphere, always encouraging others, even before I fully understood the weight and power of my own words. I can still remember family and friends whispering, "There's something special about that girl." At the time, they had no idea they were witnessing the early signs of God's favor resting on me.

My name, Althea—meaning "healer" or "wholesome"—has always felt like a prophetic mantle. Even in my youth, I had an unusual ability to bring peace where there was unrest, comfort where there was pain, and unity where there was division. My middle name, Faye, rooted in Old French and signifying "loyalty" and "belief," only added to the prophetic weight of who I was becoming. I would grow into a woman of unwavering faith and relentless loyalty to God, to my family, and to the community I was called to serve.

That Favor That Made Her

Favor is often misunderstood. Many think it is a smooth path, a shortcut to success, or a golden ticket to elevation. But my life has taught me otherwise. I have come to know that favor is often forged in the fires of adversity. My strength was not born in comfort—it was shaped in the midst of challenge. In fact, my mother faced great challenges in birthing me; even her life was at stake. Life handed me its share of trials—losses that left me breathless, including the unimaginable pain of losing two sets of twins.

But there was more.

I survived the devastation of a church fire, watching a sacred space that housed so many prayers and memories go up in flames. And if that wasn't enough, I experienced the heart-wrenching loss of both my mother and my mother-in-law, just three months apart. The grief was heavy. The silence that followed was deafening. And yet, through it all, my faith did not fade—it deepened. My resilience did not break—it sharpened. And my voice did not weaken—it grew stronger.

Where others saw tragedy, I saw God's invitation to trust Him more. In the stillness of my private pain, I learned the true meaning of favor. It is not the absence of affliction; it is the undeniable presence of God's hand holding you, steadying you, and covering you. I held tight to the words of the Psalmist: "You, Lord, bless the righteous; you surround them with your favor as with a shield" (Psalm 5:12).

Through every hardship, my faith stood firm. In fact, it was in my most broken seasons that the favor on my life became most visible. I emerged from each storm not just surviving, but transformed—wiser, more anointed, and more anchored in my divine assignment. And those around me began to notice. They could not always explain it, but they could sense it. That is what favor does—it speaks even when you do not.

A Favored Woman in Ministry

My ministry journey has been a portrait of obedience, sacrifice, and divine empowerment. As a First Lady, teacher, author, and speaker, I wear many hats, but I carry them with humility. I do not need to be the loudest in the room because I have learned that true leadership is not about volume—in fact, I prefer to blend into the background. It is about weight. My words are not just heard; they are felt because they come from a place of lived experience and divine assignment. I have become a trusted voice, not just because I speak, but because I serve. I understand what it means to be favored, and with that favor comes responsibility.

Whether I am preaching a sermon, counseling someone through grief, or working quietly behind the scenes, I know my presence carries purpose. My discernment is God-given, and my compassion runs deep. I have learned to walk in authority, never arrogance. I lead with conviction, never control. And more often than not, people walk away from an encounter with my ministry saying, "There's something different about her." I know what that difference is—it is the favor of God.

But the favor on my life is not for me alone—it is generational. It is for my daughter and every young person God has put in my life. I pour into women, into rising leaders, into those whose voices are just beginning to find their sound. I teach them to walk boldly in their callings, to embrace their own favor without fear or apology. My mentorship is rooted in wisdom, and my prayers are drenched in power. I consider myself both a midwife and a mother in the Spirit, helping others give birth to dreams they did not even know were inside them.

Favored in the Family

Beyond the pulpit and the podium, I am most favored in my role as a wife, mother, and nurturer of legacy. My marriage is more than a covenant—it is a ministry. As the wife of Bishop Shawn Bell, I have stood beside him through every mountain and every valley, always striving to walk in step with rhythm and grace. Together, we are not just partners in life, but in purpose. Our union is a testament to God's faithfulness, marked by love, unity, and divine assignment.

My children and the many spiritual sons and daughters God has entrusted to me are living evidence of the favor that flows through my life. I have worked to cultivate a home where faith is the foundation and love is non-negotiable. My family does not just see the favor of God on me—they live under its covering and benefit from its overflow. I often say, "My greatest assignment starts at home," and I mean that. I live it out daily with intentionality, grace, and a heart anchored in love.

Authorship and Voice

My literary voice has become a wellspring of healing and empowerment. Through my books, *My Scars Have a Story* and *There's a Marriage in Me,* I open the door to transparency and transformation. I write from a place of authenticity, inviting readers into my journey—not to spotlight my pain, but to reveal God's redemptive power at work in every chapter of my life.

My words are more than just testimony—they are tools. In my writing, I make it clear that favor does not mean a life free of wounds; it means having scars that testify to survival, strength, and God's sovereignty. I encourage others to see their pain not as a disqualifier, but as part of the divine process. I remind them that their purpose is greater than their past, and their story still matters. With every page I write, my favor speaks gently, powerfully, and undeniably.

The Weight of the Favored

To be favored is not to be free from responsibility. In fact, favor often comes with a weight that many never see. I know this truth intimately. My "yes" to God has cost me comfort. My obedience has led me into seasons of solitude. My calling has stretched me in ways that required courage I did not know I had. And yet, I carry the weight with grace because I have learned that favor is not for the faint of heart. It is for those willing to walk the narrow path—even when it is lonely, even when it is hard.

I have come to understand that I am not favored just for myself; I am favored for others. My life is a conduit through which God reveals His love, His strength, and His purpose. I do not stand for accolades—I stand for impact. I do not serve for applause—I serve out of assignment. And I do not give from surplus—I give from sacrifice. Because at the end of the day, to be favored is to live poured out, faithfully, and fully aligned with God's plan.

A Legacy of Favor

As I continue to walk out my journey, the favor on my life only seems to increase. I see it in the lives I have touched, in the souls I have helped lead to Christ, in the women I have empowered, and in the family I have lovingly nurtured. My legacy is not just being written in books or bios—it is being etched in the hearts of those I have poured into, mentored, prayed for, and stood beside.

I do not seek to simply be a woman of influence—I strive to be a woman of impact. I do not want to just be known—I want to be remembered. Not for titles, but for transformation. Not for visibility, but for value. I aim to be the kind of woman who reminds others of what is possible when you dare to live as one who is chosen, called, and favored by God.

Conclusion: Walking in Favor

In a world that often confuses popularity with purpose and noise with influence, I have learned to stand as a quiet storm—a woman clothed in strength and dignity, seasoned with grace, and marked by favor. My journey has taught me that favor is not about being famous; it is about being faithful. It is not measured by followers or applause, but by obedience and endurance.

To be favored is to be chosen in the fire, lifted by grace, and assigned for God's glory. I live that truth every single day. And as I continue to rise, pour, and lead, I carry others with me—especially the women who need to be reminded that favor is not something you strive for. It is something you receive. It is something you embrace.

And I am undeniably, irrevocably, and divinely… favored.

Because I've survived what others thought would break me.

Because even when the fire tried to consume the vision and grief tried to silence my praise, I kept walking.

I kept believing.

And God kept favoring.

This page intentionally left blank

About the Author

Lady A. Faye Bell is a conference speaker, spiritual midwife, author, and the First Lady of Greater Paradise Christian Center in Baltimore, Maryland. With grace, wisdom, and a deep commitment to faith, she empowers women to grow spiritually and walk confidently in their God-given purpose.

She is the published author of *My Scars Have a Story and There's a Marriage in Me,* books that reflect her passion for transparency, healing, and restoration. Through her writing and ministry, Lady Bell encourages others to embrace their journey and discover hope beyond life's challenges.

In addition to her ministry work, Lady Bell is a licensed financial advisor and lifestyle consultant, using her expertise to help individuals and families build stability and steward their resources wisely. She also serves as the Director of Women's Ministry at Greater Paradise Christian Center, where she leads initiatives designed to strengthen, equip, and inspire women in every season of life.

Despite her many accomplishments, Lady Bell considers her greatest joy to be her role as wife to Bishop Shawn L. Bell and mother to their daughter, Olivia.

Lady Bell lives and leads with the conviction that she is both called and favored, using her voice and influence to uplift others and bring glory to God.

God's Grace to Run Your Race

By Lady Detreal Mathews

Did you know that comparison is the thief of all happiness?

God does not need what we do not have. All He needs is what is left. God's eyes are searching the whole earth, looking for someone that He can add His super to their natural.

Who would you be if there was no fear, no stress, no strain, and no struggle? How would you show up? How would you move? Where would you be, and what would you be doing? God's grace is sufficient for you! Do you know that you are made in the image of God? You have intrinsic value and dignity. You are fearfully and wonderfully made; your life is intentional and precious. You are God's workmanship, and you were created with purpose and destiny. You are chosen, royal, and holy. You belong to God and are set apart. You have been given dominion, and you are made a little lower than the angels. God has placed hidden treasures inside of you. Have you come into agreement with what God says about you?

Each of us has been given a measure of faith. That faith was never supposed to be stagnant or unproductive. It was intended to increase! God has made us righteous—not through our works, but through His Son, Jesus Christ. We who are considered righteous in God's eyes live by trusting in Him and His promises, not by our own works or merit. Grace comes directly from God. It is His, and it is a gift that He gives to you and me. The phrase "God's grace" is noted approximately 170 times in the Bible. Merriam-Webster defines grace as unmerited divine assistance given to humans for their regeneration or sanctification; a virtue coming from God. Grace has a purpose, and it comes with power. It is not just given to us as an afterthought. It was well planned out by the Father so that we can be equipped with this "divine assistance." God knew that we would need this unmerited favor for the advancement of the Kingdom of God. Anything that comes directly from God is supremely good and well-orchestrated. God is a very strategic God; all His doings are well thought out.

I have learned that God's ways are not my ways, and His thoughts are not my thoughts.

Before I knew or understood God's plan for my life, I could tell that there was something "different" about me. I believed that I had the grace of God operating in my life long before I truly understood what grace really was. The way things began unfolding in my life attested to the fact that there was something bigger than me operating behind the scenes. God's grace has been shown to me through love, kindness, patience, provision, and salvation. Some things we must endure in life—whether it is God's plan for us or our own choices—but He makes us a promise that His grace is always sufficient. It is not to be taken advantage of, but to be accepted. Welcome and willingly receive the plan that God has for your life. He always desires an extraordinary life for us. Jeremiah 29:11 (KJV) says, "For I know the thoughts that I think toward you; saith the Lord, thoughts of peace and not of evil, to give you an expected end." God chooses those whom He desires.

I can remember when God's grace called my husband and me into the ministry to become pastors. I was so overwhelmed with mixed emotions and feelings of unworthiness. I fought it and was resistant to the call until I humbled myself and clearly began to hear the voice of God saying to me, "This was always the plan I had for you; you just didn't know it." God reminded me that many are called, but few are chosen. When grace calls your name, it is hard to find rest in anything until you answer.

Whenever you do not think that you are enough, God will remind you of who you really are. In our weakness is the place where God's grace meets us. His strength is made perfect in our weakness. God offers power to endure weakness so that we are able to walk through the challenging times of life. He offers the same grace to you and me that was offered to Shadrach, Meshach, and Abednego in the Book of Daniel. They were thrown into the fiery furnace, and when they came out, they were not burned, nor did they smell like smoke!

Paul reminds us in the fifth chapter of Romans that we glory in tribulations, knowing that tribulation brings patience, patience brings experience, and experience brings hope. Hoping in God will never bring disappointment because He is not a man that He should lie, nor does He repent. If God says it, you can rest assured and be confident that it will happen.

Sometimes we must be slowed down so that we can hear the truth, because the lies become so loud at times. Being slowed down sometimes looks like trials, tribulations, and tests. In those times of slowing down, it is not meant to take us out but to initiate an opportunity to begin to seek God in prayer. Some would never acknowledge Him if there was never any trouble. He will begin to whisper some things to us that we did not know. He knows the ending, the beginning, and all the in-between. Nothing catches God by surprise.

God has made us a promise that He would never put more on us than we can bear without a way of escape. Our faith allows us to come boldly to the throne of grace, that we may obtain mercy and find grace to help in time of need. We will always need the undeserved grace of God because of the imperfect people that we are. God knows how He has made us and that we are fragile. It is by the grace of God that we are who we are. He is the All-Sufficient One, not us. All our talents, abilities, and callings are a direct result of God's grace. These are the things that God makes possible for us. God's grace alone does not guarantee success because not all people will put faith in God's grace. We must put faith with God's grace to release its power. We must labor against the flesh to rest in God's grace (Wommack, 1996). The forethought of who we would become was not only for God's use, but also for those who are connected to us.

The grace of God is a locator, and it is looking for someone to shower with transformative power. One of my favorite scriptures is 2 Chronicles 16:9a (KJV): "The eyes of the Lord search the whole earth in order to strengthen those whose hearts are fully committed to him." Another translation says that He is looking for someone to show Himself strong to. It's not just someone—it is you and me that His eyes are looking for.

When God strengthens us, it's not just to become physically strong, but that strength looks like inner peace amid chaos. You might be in the middle of a storm—grief, stress, loss, or fear—but still feel a kind of calm that does not make logical sense. It looks like endurance you did not know you had. There are times when you look back and wonder how you kept going. That's God's strength sustaining you. God's strength might look like the courage to speak up, forgive, let go, or face something terrifying. It's not that the fear disappears; it's that you are given strength to move forward in spite of it. Even after disappointment or failure, God can restore your hope. That hope is a form of strength, and it helps you get up again.

The Word of God says, "If you are willing and obedient, you shall eat the good of the land." God gives us a choice between life and death, blessings and curses. We make this choice by loving the Lord, obeying

Him, and committing ourselves to Him. There is a grace that is provided to us that empowers us to be obedient. Grace empowers you through the Holy Spirit. God's grace doesn't just forgive you when you fall; it gives you strength not to fall. That power comes from the Holy Spirit working in you, not from trying harder on your own. God's grace will do for you that which you cannot do for yourself.

Grace changes your heart, not just your behavior. When you receive God's grace, you begin to want what He wants. Obedience becomes less about duty and more about desire, because grace rewires your heart to love God. Obedience flows from relationship. When you're close to God, you are more aligned with His will, and obedience becomes natural. Obedience is a journey, and we all stumble. But grace means that failure is not the end. God's grace gives you the courage to get back up and keep trusting Him.

About the Author

Lady Detreal Mathews, born and raised in Alexandria, Louisiana, now resides in Crosby, Texas. She is a devoted wife, mother, and grandmother whose life reflects a deep faith in God and a sincere passion for serving others.

Professionally, Lady Mathews works as a Licensed Chemical Dependency Counselor, where her compassionate and empathetic nature allows her to help individuals and families find freedom, healing, and restoration. Her work reflects her commitment to guiding others toward wholeness and renewed hope.

Lady Mathews faithfully serves alongside her husband in ministry at By Faith Ministries International of Baytown, where she supports the mission of the church and contributes to the spiritual development of the congregation. Together, they model servant leadership and are dedicated to strengthening families, nurturing spiritual growth, and bringing positive transformation to their community.

Through both her professional and ministry work, Lady Mathews continues to encourage others to walk in faith, healing, and purpose.

Heart Issues

by *Lady Rhoda Williams*

"Create in me a clean heart, O God, and renew a right spirit within me."
—Psalm 51:10

The "heart" in biblical terms is the core of human will, emotions, and intellect. The heart is where all the issues of life flow. The Bible says in Proverbs 4:23, "Keep thy heart with all diligence; for out of it are the issues of life." In other words, we are to be mindful of our inner self—our thoughts, emotions, and desires. We often relate heart issues to physical ailments (a physical disorder or illness), but today we are going to deal with the spiritual side of the heart—issues relating to inner thoughts, upbringing, hurts from the past, negative words spoken over you, and bad decisions, just to name a few. We are looking at how these issues, if left unchecked, turn into low self-esteem, insecurity, an unforgiving heart, bitterness, or rage. These are the life issues we hide behind. These are heart issues that have the potential to keep you in unhealthy relationships or searching for love in people, places, or things. It's these small, but giant, issues you face daily that will hinder your relationship with God.

You do not have to go another second, another day, or another year not knowing who you are in Christ Jesus. Most of us are familiar with the book of Psalms. We have heard the teachings of King David and how he was a man after God's own heart, but he had "heart issues." He had things he had to keep at the foot of the cross. But one thing about King David—he knew where his help came from. He knew the only One who could deliver him from his issues was the Almighty God. That's why throughout the book of Psalms David was always crying out to God, and David was real and upfront about his heart issues. Read the book of Psalms for heartfelt prayers from David.

Growing up, I was raised by a single mother struggling to raise six children on her own. My mom didn't have time to show love or affection. She was too busy trying to make sure we had food on the table, clothes on our backs, and a roof over our heads. We didn't experience the two-parent home where the father worked and the mother took care of the home. Don't get me wrong—I understand now how God uses everything (the good, the bad, and the ugly) for our good (Romans 8:28). I am the woman I am today because of a strong mother who never gave up on life.

We all have issues we face when we reach adulthood. I truly believe it is all part of the process for God to shape and mold us into the person He created us to be. The Bible says in Psalm 51:5, "Behold, I was shapen in iniquity; and in sin did my mother conceive me." In other words, don't count it strange when you find yourself in unfamiliar places. We don't know how much we need to change until we are face-to-face with our Heavenly Father. As a young girl with a stuttering problem, I was always afraid to speak in front of others, which led to low self-esteem. I didn't feel good about myself, which led to insecurity. I had a lot of resentment toward my mom, which led to unforgiveness. These were all heart issues I experienced, and now I had issues with men, issues with speaking in public, and trust issues, just to name a few.

Like King David, I wanted a change. So I began to cry out to God, and He heard my cry (Psalm 18:6). God gave me a three-step recovery process that changed my life. When you think about recovery, we often think addictions—but we're not talking about being addicted to drugs or alcohol. I'm talking about recovering from sin, insecurity, low self-esteem, fear, doubt, unbelief, and ourselves. These things will hinder your walk with God. I was insecure, had low self-esteem, and was afraid of being alone, and therefore I settled for anything and anyone. I wanted better for myself and my children, but I didn't know how to get there. Until one day, God gave me this recovery process that I pray will change your life and draw you closer to God. To start the recovery process, you must have an action plan.

Remember, we're talking about heart issues—the small, unchecked issues that keep you in unhealthy relationships.

Step One: Pray

The first thing I learned how to do was pray. This simple act of obedience will draw you into a closer and more enjoyable relationship with God. I say simple because prayer is simply you communicating with God daily. You must include prayer in your daily routine until it becomes a lifestyle. Just like getting dressed in the morning—we dress physically, and we must clothe ourselves spiritually (Ephesians 6:10–18).

We talked about David and how he had a heart after God, but David also had a prayer life. During your time of prayer is where God shows you those unchecked heart issues. This is the time to be open with God so the healing process can begin. God is love, and He wants to shape and mold you into the person He created you to be. But you must commit to doing things God's way, and it starts with prayer.

In your quiet time with God, He will give you clear instructions on what to do. When you read the story of Noah in Genesis 6:14, God told Noah exactly what to do and how to do it. When your heart is open to receive, you will hear clear instructions from God. So get yourself a journal and be ready to write down those instructions. Be ready to put what you read and hear into practice.

Step Two: Just Believe

Your next step in the recovery process is to believe God. Whatever God tells you to do—do it. Luke 5:4–5 says, "When he had finished speaking, he said to Simon, 'Now go out where it is deep, and let down your nets to catch some fish.' 'Master,' Simon replied, 'we worked hard all night and didn't catch a thing. But if you say so, I'll let the nets down again.'"

I hear you: "I have tried everything under the sun to get things right in my life." "I am sick and tired of being sick and tired." "It didn't work the last time." But this time around is going to be different. This time you are going to do things God's way. Matthew 21:22 says, "If you believe, you will receive." I'm not talking about receiving material things—I'm talking about healing those heart issues.

Imagine for a moment Jesus standing in front of you asking you this simple question: "What do you want from me?" What do you desperately need God to do for you today? Let's look at the story in Mark 10. Blind Bartimaeus had a need, and Jesus asked him a simple question: "What do you want me to do?" Bartimaeus had a need, and he was not going to miss his opportunity to be healed. He quickly answered Jesus and said, "I want to see!" Don't miss this opportunity to have the life you desire. This time around—trust God!

Step Three: Faith

Faith must be accompanied by action. As you read Genesis 7:1–5, Noah did exactly as the Lord commanded. Things will never change in your life until you do something about it. Noah could have sat around and believed what God said, but he took it a step further and acted on what he heard. He did exactly what God instructed him to do and built the ark. We complicate things when we don't do things God's way. The

Bible says you are a new person in Christ. No more looking back—keep moving forward.

I believe things are changing for you right now. Your faith is increasing, and you are going to do things God's way. Give those heart issues to God and watch Him work things out for your good.

Let's Finalize This

To deal with your heart issues, you must have an action plan. The Bible says in James 2:14–26 that faith without works is dead.

Recovery Process:

- Find a church home (Hebrews 10:24–25).
- Change your confession; watch what comes out of your mouth (Proverbs 18:21).
- Surround yourself with other believers (Proverbs 13:20).
- Start a consistent prayer life (1 Thessalonians 5:17) and read the Word daily (Joshua 1:8).
- Stop hanging around the things and people who are causing you to fall back into your old life (1 Corinthians 15:33).
- Build a meaningful life with God (Matthew 6:33).

And finally, don't give up on yourself. You will never know the power of God's Word if you quit. Keep repeating steps 1, 2, and 3 until it becomes a lifestyle.

About the Author

Lady Rhoda Williams, is a compassionate teacher and ministry leader who serves as the co-founder and vice president of New Season Christian Church in Indiana. The church is a loving ministry dedicated to helping individuals experience a fresh start and discover the hope of a new beginning in Christ.

Under the leading of God, Lady Rhoda published her first book, It's Just That Simple, a daily devotional that explores the practical and transformative truths found in God's Word. Through her writing, she encourages readers to embrace the simplicity and power of a life rooted in faith.

Lady Rhoda is a cum laude graduate of Indiana Wesleyan University, where she earned her Bachelor of Science degree in Business Administration. Her educational background, combined with her heart for ministry, equips her to serve with wisdom, leadership, and compassion.

She has been married to Pastor Rodney Williams for over 27 years, and together they have been blessed with three children and eight grandchildren. Lady Rhoda continues to serve faithfully in ministry, using her gifts to uplift others and point them toward a life renewed by God's grace.

IGNITE THE FLAME
A Pastor's Wife and the Fire of Revival

By Lady Janis Drayton

As the Pastor's wife, we are not only called to serve by putting out fires, but also to help fan the flames of revival! Woman of God, know that you carry both God's love and fire. You possess not only the capacity to stand under His anointed power, but also the grace to be that spark in dead, dry places. We fan the flames of revival that help prevent others from becoming stagnant in their faith, bound in religious traditions, or stuck in unhealthy cycles. But to be that spark, we ourselves have to be burning!

Beholding Him — Prayer, Worship, and a Surrendered Life

We've often heard, "You are what you eat!" If you only consume junk food, eventually your body will bear the fruit of the seeds sown into it. The same holds true for what we focus on. To "behold" means to stop, look, and perceive. In my husband's early days of pastoring, my emotions were constantly in turmoil because I was always overwhelmed with what I saw week to week. I saw people's imperfections, their disrespect, their weaknesses, and myself being rejected constantly. I often missed the move of God in services because I was mistakenly distracted by what the enemy wanted me to see!

It is imperative that we do not become distracted by what the enemy highlights. Either intentionally or unintentionally, people we serve will disappoint us, hurt us, or be unappreciative in some capacity. It's the nature of the flesh! However, I challenge you to be deliberate in rejecting the enemy's strategically planted shadows that deceive you from seeing God. We should always be praying for God to give us eyes to see what He is revealing so we can properly respond.

My husband once said to me, "When you keep your gaze on God instead of the enemy, if needed, He'll show you the enemy!" So, my sister, don't waste your gaze! You won't miss anything that is meant for you to see. Instead, behold the Father, knowing He is doing an active work in you. Second Corinthians 3:18 shares, "And we, who with unveiled faces all reflect the Lord's glory, are being transformed into His likeness with ever-increasing glory, which comes from the Lord, who is the Spirit." Simply put, we become what we behold!

This change won't have to be announced, but will be clearly seen by others. "Those who look to Him are radiant!" (Psalm 34:5). Beholding Him is not being blind to encountered challenges, but setting your heart's posture to see Him in everything. See His glory, fire, and love for you first, and then for others. Having a personal revelation of Christ positions us to truly respond with a surrendered life where worship begins in our lifestyle, not just in the sanctuary. Beholding God pivots every part of our life toward Him. Here your prayers mature, responses to challenges are tempered, your ministry offers up a pleasing fragrance, and through you people are drawn to His glory.

If you want to ignite hunger and thirst in others, become hungry for Him yourself! "Go into your secret place and pray to your Father" (Matthew 6:6), and live your life with a complete dependence upon Him. There's no secret formula for this transformative power, only the Secret Place (Psalm 91:1). Under His shadow is the place we run to for revelation, protection, and transformation. I challenge you, First Lady, to become fascinated with your God. Practice being content in His presence, and guard your personal time with Him as if your life depends on it—because it does!

Disciple People with Fire and Not Programs

We are living in a time of self-empowerment and individualized truths. Everyone is looking for solutions and the easiest pathway to a fulfilled life. This reality is also in your church, and it can be easy for us as leaders to become pressured into people-pleasing and program managing in order to attract or keep people satisfied in our congregations. However, we are the church, not a glorified social club with self-help groups or quick-fix clinics.

I have learned that tea parties, book clubs, and prayer breakfasts are good, but can only take people so far. We have a responsibility to provide people a pathway to the Father. Programs and events will not change behaviors in people when there is no heart change. The Spirit conforms the heart. Our activities and great ideas may help people feel better, but it is God's fire that purifies us into change!

Jesus said, "I have come to bring fire on the earth, but oh how I wish it were already kindled!" (Luke 12:49).

I remember when attending my son's kindergarten open house, one parent asked about nap time, and the teacher's response was, "There's too much for us to learn to have nap time!" I feel this is the same today. We have men, women, and children coming to our churches who are battling sickness, confused identities, abusive relationships, financial ruin, and struggles with their faith and God's love for them. We cannot afford to offer the failed remedies of the world.

People need the fire of God! He alone has power to heal, deliver, refine, and irreversibly change their lives and circumstances. We must remember the souls placed in our care are not there to make us feel good, important, or validated. We are there to ensure every opportunity we have in their presence shows them the love of the Father and His fire! Let us be that spark in their lives that ignites an irrevocable change!

Second Timothy 1:6 says, "For this reason I remind you to fan into flame the gift of God." Every Bible study, prayer service, and staff meeting should be impactful and intentional. Everything we do should be covered in intercession and fire! We intercede for the cause of supernatural impact in their lives. It is from Abba's heart that we lead. "He who ministers from his heart seeks his own glory, but the one who seeks the glory of the One who sent him is true, and no unrighteousness is in him, and he will not miss his target."

We ignite cold, dark places with the fire of God and should always resolve to seek God's heart before we approach anything in ministry. Whether preaching, teaching, hosting an event, or planning a program, we pray that the heart and fire of God will always reach its intended target!

Know that revival is not an event, but a lifestyle set to burn with a continual rhythm of changed hearts, renewed minds, holy living, and passion for God.

Be the Watchman and the Fireplace!

Heat, fuel, and oxygen are all needed to ignite and sustain a fire. Remove any one of these and the fire goes out. As the Pastor's wife, you play a vital role in helping to guard the ignited fire in the hearts of those you serve. Isaiah 62:6 says, "I have posted watchmen on your walls, Jerusalem;

they will never be silent day and night. You who call on the Lord, give yourselves no rest."

Three things to be aware of:

1. The enemy does not want revival!
2. The enemy does not want us in the Secret Place!
3. The enemy does not want us to be strong in faith!

It is important that we, as Pastor's wives, position ourselves high—not in the sanctuary, but on the wall! We must be a watchman for the community we've been called to serve. We go high so we can watch for the attack of the enemy. In Nehemiah, revival was occurring, and he placed watchmen high on the wall and gatekeepers at the gates below. The watchmen were looking out for the enemy and the move of God! They were to sound the alarm from the wall so that the people could respond accordingly.

Watchmen could discern the enemy from afar, see gaps and vulnerable spaces in the walls, check for fires, and give directions to the gatekeepers below. Watchmen were able to see from afar what could not yet be seen on ground level. When the Pastor's wife's heart is postured above, God will send dreams, visions, and words of knowledge and wisdom that alert and speak to the present season and announce new ones.

It is essential to keep our eyes fixed on what the Holy Spirit is showing us and not on the foolishness occurring at surface levels. God will instruct when to pray, when to warn, and when to give hope. We have to stay in the Secret Place and grow in wisdom when managing relationships we entertain, activities we partake in, and the private time we set with God.

Habakkuk 2:1 says, "I will stand my watch, set myself on the rampart, and watch to see what He will say to me, and what I will answer." As watchmen of the house, we should devote ourselves to intercession, being watchful and thankful. We intercede with boldness knowing that He hears us. We need not be ashamed, for the blood of Christ grants us access.

As trailblazers, we clear paths for what others will walk in publicly, and we push back the kingdom of darkness from the territory God has given to us. We guard the spirit of revival just as we would a fire needed to keep our homes warm. Like a fireplace, we create space for God in everything we do. We fuel ourselves in His Word and devote ourselves to prayer, providing oxygen and life so Holy Ghost fire is raging in us, in our congregation, and in this world!

Revival isn't ignited by a title, but by a life set ablaze. When the Pastor's wife burns for God, the whole house begins to feel the heat!

This page intentionally left blank

About the Author

Lady Janis Drayton, is a pastor's wife of sixteen years with a deep passion for revival, spiritual growth, and the restoration of God's people. She faithfully serves in ministry by leading Women's Ministry, teaching Sunday School, and investing in the spiritual development of others through teaching and discipleship.

Janis is also a certified Biblical Counselor and a National Board-Certified Health and Wellness Coach (NBC-HWC). Through these roles, she helps individuals pursue both spiritual and personal wholeness, encouraging them to live healthy and balanced lives grounded in biblical truth.

Married for twenty-four years, Janis is a devoted wife and the proud mother of two. She currently resides in Williamsville, New York, where she continues to serve her local church and community with compassion and dedication.

Janis' greatest passion is to see women healed, empowered, and walking confidently in their God-given purpose. Her life and ministry reflect a deep love for God and a sincere commitment to serving His people with grace and truth.

Justice, Judas, Jealousy, Jezebel, Joy

Discerning the Wisdom and Beauty in God's Justice: Dethroning Jezebel, Guarding Against Judas, Overcoming Jealousy, and Experiencing Joy as God's Leading Lady

By Apostle Scharita Lacey

Introduction

The role of the First Lady has been that of a proverbial woman, a quintessential leader who embodies faith, fragrance, wisdom, kindness, love, purpose, and intentionality. The First Lady is expected to be kind, understanding, accommodating, and caring; to understand protocol and decorum; to love God, her husband, her children, and her family; and to serve the members of the ministry and church.

The First Lady has to learn to adjust—to be the greatest adapter—to be able to "pull through," to show the greatest restraint under fire and pressure while demonstrating the greatest amount of personal resiliency. The First Lady has to be visibly "seen," although she is not always "understood," and somewhere between trying to demonstrate her love for her husband, her dedication to her God, and her commitment to the church and ministry, if she is not careful, she can lose herself—her identity, her image, her voice, her light.

When the light of the First Lady goes dim, it is usually the result of a spiritual test, trial, or attack that she has experienced.

Warfare

Warfare is a position that each First Lady will come to understand and witness, where distress, pressure, and the weight of what she carries attempt to collapse her and take her under.

In these moments of opposition, great testing, and great trials, if the First Lady does not have proper grounding, the inner work of the Holy Spirit, a strong foundation in the Word of God, and a support community, she may succumb to the pressures of spiritual attack.

The First Lady must understand how to navigate spiritual warfare and discern God's justice.

Dethroning Jezebel & Exposing Judas

Every First Lady, at some point during her time being married to a pastor, will experience the misfortune of Jezebel behaviors and systems that seek to attack and destroy her marriage, their ministry, her family, her integrity, character, and name.

Oftentimes, these individuals operating in a spirit of Jezebel will weaponize their influence, their possessions, and their access in a way that seeks to gain control over the leader (her husband).

As a pastor's wife, you must not be ignorant of the games that individuals operating in this spirit play, the level of confusion and disorder they cause, and the spirit of divination, rebellion, and witchcraft in which they operate.

The Jezebel system as a whole is a great danger to the First Lady's marriage, home, and peace. It can even be a danger to her life, physically and spiritually, if the legalities are not exposed and properly dealt with.

Jezebel must be managed. Not every member or family member can be cut off or disassociated, which means the pastor's wife has to possess great wisdom and discernment for navigating those who operate with a spirit of divination and rebellion.

Jezebel Checklist

- Likes to be the center of attention
- Seeks to be in authority and have influence
- Rarely takes accountability
- Always blames and passes judgment
- Operates in secrecy, withholding key information from the leader
- Avoids the First Lady
- Usurps authority in decision-making
- Places idols

There will be a Judas in every ministry. This person will operate in a spirit of retaliation, false witness, and with a bad heart.

There is a difference between wayward members and leaders and those who possess bad hearts.

Jesus knew that Judas would betray Him, but He kept him close because He allowed Judas to reveal himself.

As hard as this is for the First Lady to hear, the Judas in your life, ministry, and circles is playing their part. Your personal job is not to allow Judas' heart to change yours—to remove all bitterness, fear, frustration, and desires for revenge.

The Lord will anchor you, sustain you, and give you wisdom and hope when navigating individuals with poor character and bad hearts. The Holy Spirit, who discerns motives, will reveal what is there and how to proceed forward.

Protect your peace.

Don't go fighting every Jezebel and Judas in your ministry. Learn how to guard and protect your marriage, family, ministry, and your peace.

When you have to deploy a strategy, God will give you the wisdom of what to do, how to do it, what to say to your husband (the pastor), and how to pray.

When spiritual warfare is waging, the First Lady's assignment is to pray and to be filled with the aroma and fragrance of heaven.

You can't afford to be caught off guard in spiritual attacks, battles, tests, and warfare.

Rest, stay fit, worship, pray, and stay engaged in what the Word is over the House and ministry—how God is leading your space—and be aware of things or individuals that may be disrupting His peace, His Spirit, and causing distress or emotional pain or trauma.

Signs of Jezebel and Judas Infiltration in a Ministry

- Lack of sleep
- Membership decline
- False ideology / theology / heresy
- Membership divided
- Illegal alliances
- Rebellion against leadership
- Spirit of divination
- Lack of prayer and consecration; no power in the ministry
- No harvest of souls
- Attacks against the senior leader and the First Family
- Cycles of death and financial ruin in the ministry or family
- Loss of opportunities and business deals

Spouse Signs

- Lack of sleep
- Health challenges

- Bewilderment and inability to focus
- Difficulty hearing a word from God for himself or the sheep
- Lack of productivity (inability to create)

Pray, consecrate, anoint, and cover your husband.

Your marriage and family are under attack.

Guard the borders of your home, the ministry, and your marriage with prayer. Ensure that there are intercessors in the ministry who pray, consecrate, and fast for you, your husband, your children, and your family to strengthen the borders and the walls.

Don't allow those who operate in the spirit of Jezebel or with the heart of Judas to steal your joy and peace.

Declarations

- My husband will live and will not die prematurely from the stress of leading the ministry.
- My husband is healthy and lives in God's peace.
- Every Jezebel and Judas has been disempowered, disallowed, and dethroned.
- Righteous men and women are assigned to my husband's destiny and life and to help us build.

Romans 13:8 (KJV)

"Owe no man any thing, but to love one another: for he that loveth another hath fulfilled the law."

Micah 6:8 (KJV)

"He hath shewed thee, O man, what is good; and what doth the LORD require of thee, but to do justly, and to love mercy, and to walk humbly with thy God?"

Guarding Against Jealousy

Jealousy will eat away at the soul of the leading lady.

There will be women in her ministry who are jealous of her influence, her personality, her style, her looks, and the way she dresses.

There will be women who judge her because she doesn't act like a First Lady. She doesn't look like a First Lady. She doesn't behave like a First Lady, and she doesn't meet their expectations.

If you're not careful and you don't guard your heart, jealousy will erode your soul. Jealousy will try to minimize your impact and influence and make you feel small.

It is important that, as a leading lady, you rest assured in the beauty, bravery, and brilliance of who you are and whose you are—outside of being your husband's wife, outside of being the leading lady and First Lady of the church and ministry, and outside of being your children's mother.

You must know that you are a daughter of the Most High God and that you walk with power and authority, with your head held high.

Your primary call is that of a daughter of God, and you are seated as a daughter of God. That is your highest calling and your greatest honor.

In addition to that, that is your husband. You are there to care for him, serve with him, nurture him, love him, and be what he needs you to be. You do not have to meet the expectations of anyone else.

Jealousy will come from unusual places.

Women will snark and do all sorts of petty things and misbehave in an effort to show you that they don't like you, that they are jealous of your personality, your hair, your looks, your beauty, and the way you love.

This is not anything that you should allow to make you feel inferior or affect your self-esteem.

It is important to have a very healthy self-image as a leading lady.

Remember—you are modeling.

Other women are watching you: the young woman, the middle-aged woman, and the older woman. Most importantly, your husband and children are watching you.

They need to see you as resilient. They need to see you as kind. They need to see you as loving.

Jealousy should never be in your heart, even when you feel like a woman is competing for your husband's attention.

You must guard your heart.

You must guard your words.

You must guard your tongue.

You must be secure in your identity and create a space where everyone feels loved, valued, celebrated, and appreciated.

As you, the leading lady and the pastor's wife, create an environment of honor, celebration, and transparency, other women will do the same when they are able to take the mask down, be sisters, and operate in the spirit of love instead of jealousy and competition.

Justice

God's justice looks like this:

"I, the Lord, will repay trouble with trouble for those who trouble you."

Turn your eyes toward Jesus.

Get out of the flesh.

See them as a soul.

Pray for them.

Love mercy.

Serve the vision.

Serve your husband.

Serve God's people.

Have a heart for justice. Love what God loves and allow Him to fight your battles.

Your husband will defend your honor, and God will.

2 Thessalonians 1:6 (KJV)

"Seeing it is a righteous thing with God to recompense tribulation to them that trouble you."

Isaiah 30:15 (KJV)

"For thus saith the Lord GOD, the Holy One of Israel;
In returning and rest shall ye be saved;
in quietness and in confidence shall be your strength."

Joy

Joy is the antidote for mourning, and the Bible says that He will take off the garment of heaviness and give you the spirit of praise.

Being a pastor's wife, being a First Lady, being a leading lady of a church and ministry is no easy chore. It is a holy and sacred calling. It is a commissioning, and it is something that God equips you to do and build with as you grow with your mate.

Some pastors' wives come into this calling when their husband is already pastoring. Some marry their husband and then learn about the call that God has on his life.

Either way, God has equipped the pastor's wife with the tools and the abilities she needs to support her husband and to be an asset to the ministry.

It is a great honor and a high esteem to serve as the leading lady, to serve God's people, and to build the Kingdom in this way.

Within this calling, the First Lady is clothed in honor, walks in humility, and is not ashamed to reveal her humanity. She is a woman given to righteous character, conduct, and behavior.

She understands that her role is sacred, but she also understands that she is human—and that God meets her in both.

The pastor's wife's joy is restored through worship, prayer, kindness, love, and a nurturing environment.

The Lord promises to refresh and restore your soul as you make your habitation in Him and place your cares in Him.

Joy will exude from you.

Joy will be in your laughter, your hugs to others, your sweet smile, and the kindness that you display to the women, men, children, and families that you lead and serve as a pastor's wife.

It is important to know that joy is a fruit of the Spirit, and it must be nurtured in your personal life, in your home, in your marriage, and in the ministry that you help to serve and lead.

Not every pastor's wife will be called to be a co-pastor, an assistant pastor, an executive pastor, the children's ministry pastor, the worship pastor, or even the women's ministry director, but every pastor's wife has a special touch.

She has what is needed for the House.

Embrace your signature authenticity that brings you joy.

God has equipped you.

Joy is your portion.

About the Author

Apostle Scharita Lacey, is an Author, Visionary, Life Coach, and Philanthropist. She leads an international movement to inspire and empower the lives of women around the globe through The Virtuous Women's Network (VWN).

She holds a Bachelor of Science in Business Administration, a Master of Business Administration, and a Master of Arts in Human Services Counseling, and is a certified life and marriage coach.

As the founder of Ignite Hope A NJ Nonprofit, she supports families affected by autism, provides resources for women in crisis and transition, and mentors college-aged women.

She resides in New Jersey, where she leads Life Worship Ministries and is ordained as an apostle, prophet, and pastor.

Her life's mission is to empower others to embrace healing, walk in freedom, and pursue their God-given purpose.

Connect

Website: www.sleglobal.net

Facebook and Instagram: @sleglobal

Email: admin@sleglobal.net

K.N.O.W.
Knowledge, Nurture, Operate, Walk

By Dr. Diane Duckett

It feels like just yesterday when I, filled with excitement, embarked on a new chapter in my ministry life. This was no ordinary ministry; it was a calling that would lead my husband and me away from a ministry we deeply loved to something entirely different—something God had specifically asked us to initiate. Admittedly, the transition was a challenging one, but we understood it was necessary and thus began a journey that promised both fulfillment and struggle.

In those initial months of building a new church from the ground up, everything seemed to fall into place perfectly. We were on a roll, and soon people began to come, drawn by the inspiring work God was revealing through us. It didn't take long before our cozy basement venue became too small to accommodate our growing congregation. The moment we opened the doors to our new building was electric—God was undeniably at work, and we were overwhelmed by the response. Yet, as more individuals joined our ministry, I noticed my husband becoming increasingly engrossed in his role, dedicating himself to others while I seemed to fade into the background.

I began to feel like I was merely getting the scraps of his attention, the leftovers of his time and love. It was a sentiment many First Ladies likely recognize, and it stung. The ministry started to bloom larger than our relationship, and the joy I once found in this calling spiraled into resentment. Weariness set in, whispering temptations in my ear to abandon it all, to throw in the towel and simply walk away. Deep down, however, I knew that wouldn't be the answer. I couldn't just leave behind the people who needed my unique gift.

Realizing I needed a change in perspective, I shifted my focus inward. Instead of fretting over my husband's involvement in the ministry, I turned my attention to myself and the specific purpose God had placed within me. As I began to navigate this path of self-awareness, I felt a gentle urging within my spirit: "Know who you are and recognize the significance of the gift you carry." This gift, I understood, was essential— not just for me, but for the Kingdom and those yearning for it.

In response, I took the time to isolate myself from the overwhelming outside influences, aiming to truly understand my identity and the unique calling on my life. This marked the beginning of a profound journey toward self-awareness—one that I thought I already knew, but this time I understood would change everything. It was a moment that called for deep reflection. I knew it wasn't enough to simply exist; I needed to truly know myself—the essence of who I was and the unique gifts I had to offer the world. So I embarked on a quest of self-awareness, eager to uncover every facet of my being—the beauty, the flaws, and even the shadows.

In this journey, I posed a pivotal question to myself: *What does it truly mean to know oneself?* I learned that self-awareness is the compass guiding us through life's intricate maze. It's a spiritual adventure—an exploration of our own identity and our purpose here on earth. As I navigated this path, I realized that understanding the depths of who I am is not just essential; it is liberating. When I peeled back the layers and faced my authentic self, my perspective transformed. It changed the way I received information and how I viewed people, places, and things. No longer would I fret over what I lacked; instead, I would come to appreciate the unique contributions I had to offer—the gift that I carry—and embrace my uniqueness by diving into the essence of me.

To truly understand who I am, I realized I needed to seek knowledge and wisdom. Every day I would pray, "God, reveal to me what it is I need to know." I believe that the Bible teaches us that God gives us wisdom. He speaks knowledge and understanding into our lives. Scripture reminds us, "For the LORD giveth wisdom: out of his mouth cometh knowledge and understanding," as stated in Proverbs 2:6 (KJV). I discovered that knowledge is indeed powerful. Understanding this required me to commit to changing my mindset, being transformed by the renewing of my mind, and engaging deeply with myself—exploring the vastness of my being.

Studying my differences and studying who I really was, and the unique gift that I carried, became a priority. As I began this journey of self-awareness, everything started to transform. I began to see myself through a new lens, immersing myself in the rich, fresh experiences that reflected who I was truly meant to be. Each revelation from God's Word, coupled with spending time praying and meditating deeply, added layers to my connection with self, making it richer and more vibrant. It encouraged me to embrace my uniqueness even more. I believe when you embark on your own quest for knowledge, you will uncover a treasure—a jewel that's been waiting to be found by you, just for you. This is why knowledge of yourself is powerful in understanding your uniqueness.

As I gained knowledge of who I am, I then had to nurture who I am. Nurturing is a gift. The more you nurture, the more you grow. It's like taking care of a plant. If you don't nurture or water the plant, it will wither and eventually die. I had to nurture the treasure I tapped into. I had to water what I learned about myself and live in the moment of my newfound awareness, creating more space for growth. This meant I had to intentionally pour into myself spiritually, mentally, and emotionally—watering me by using "I AM" affirmations to build up and not tear down, journaling my experiences, and praising my way through it.

I had to create space to nurture the gift I was carrying and learn where my gift grows the most. Just like a plant, all plants do not grow in the same environment. Some require sunlight, some require shade, some grow outside, some inside, and others may require both. But for each plant to grow properly, you must learn where it grows the most. The gift that I carry can grow in multiple environments. It's not just for a specific place, but for multiple spaces and places. Psalm 1:3 (KJV) states, "And he shall be like a tree planted by the rivers of water, that bringeth forth his fruit in his season; his leaf also shall not wither; and whatsoever he doeth shall prosper." The gift that you carry—don't let it die, but be determined to nurture it so that it can grow. Water it, feed it, cover it—nurture you. Nurture the gift in you. As you nurture it, it will grow and produce fruit in its season.

Once I gained knowledge and nurtured who I am, I began to operate in who I am. I started to live in alignment with my newfound mindset, making it a priority to be true to myself. No longer am I defined by someone else's identity; instead, I am operating in my authentic self. Every day presents the opportunity to become who I was meant to be—the person God created me to be. Acknowledging and embracing what I now know about myself and my gifts has truly transformed my life. It has sharpened my focus and allowed me to make a meaningful impact in the lives of others because I finally recognize the value I carry. As 1 Peter 4:10 (AMP) beautifully puts it, "Just as each one of you has received a special gift [spiritual talent, an ability graciously given by God], employ it in serving one another."

Finally, I needed to walk in and embrace who I truly am. I recognized the unique gift I carry and aligned my life with God's will. I refused to let setbacks or distractions take over my focus any longer. I learned to breathe deeply, connecting with the essence of my true self. As I began to walk in my authenticity, I noticed more opportunities opening up for me. It felt incredible to step through those doors, fully aware of who I am and the gift I carry.

It's like Ephesians 4:1 (NKJV) says, "to walk worthy of the calling with which you were called, with all lowliness and gentleness, with longsuffering, bearing with one another in love." Walking in knowing who you are is like walking in the woods—embracing all that it entails: lowliness, gentleness, and longsuffering, while walking in your awareness with purpose, reflecting on all that you have learned about who you are, and making a difference wherever you arrive.

Understanding who I am comes from self-awareness, nurturing my growth, adopting a new mindset, and truly walking in my identity. This journey has been about coming to **KNOW** who I really am.

About the Author

Dr. Diane Duckett is a dedicated leader and co-founder of New Kingdom Faith Christian Church in Glen Burnie, Maryland, where she serves alongside her husband in ministry. She is not only a preacher and teacher, but also a motivational speaker, coach, and entrepreneur who has a deep passion for Jesus Christ. Her enthusiasm inspires many to develop a closer relationship with Christ and to truly know Him.

In addition to her ministry work, Dr. Diane is the founder and owner of I AM Success Life Coach, LLC. As a certified Success and Transformational Life Coach, she empowers individuals to reach their full potential in both their personal lives and professional endeavors.

Through her ministry and coaching, Dr. Duckett remains committed to helping others grow spiritually, discover their purpose, and walk confidently in the life God has called them to live.

The Weight of Loyalty

By Dr. Kecia Reed

Loyalty is a word that carries an immeasurable amount of weight, yet it is handled so carelessly because of a lack of understanding. Too many equate loyalty with what and how a person treats another individual, but after much prayer and meditation, I have come to a heartfelt discovery: loyalty is driven by a person of heart.

According to the dictionary, loyalty is a steadfast commitment of the heart, mind, and actions to a person, purpose, or covenant. It is marked by faithfulness, integrity, and endurance, even in the face of adversity, temptation, or personal cost. As you can see, this seven-letter word is weighty.

Before I go into greater explanation about loyalty, I want to mention that there's a song by Sam Cooke that says, "It's been a long, a long time coming, but I know a change gon' come." I believe those lyrics—raw, resilient, and prophetic—do more than echo through our speakers; they speak volumes to the hearts of those such as myself who have labored in silence, interceded without applause, and held fast to a call without reservation. A change was going to come. Sam Cooke's melody is Heaven's whisper to a group of women that change is not only coming, but it is demanding our agreement.

Loyalty Prerequisite

Loyalty is no longer negotiable. It is not performance-driven. It is not selective obedience dressed up as spiritual maturity. Loyalty is a heart posture; it is a mirror that reflects either the humility of Christ or the self-interest of flesh. In the Kingdom, loyalty doesn't wear masks. It weeps at altars, wrestles through obedience, and remains when betrayal makes staying feel unbearable. The oil of loyalty is costly, but it is holy. It is the signature of a life surrendered.

Loyalty must be at the root because it is the foundation upon which consistency is built. Loyalty has been speculated to be found in organizations, marriages, sororities, women's social groups, and church cliques, only for many to join or be a part and discover the disharmony among most of the affiliates.

Just note, in all honesty, being part of organizations is not bad because we all need community, but it is the disharmony that is projected that reveals loyalty is not just the right hand of fellowship—it truly is the undertone of the heart. Let me support my thought with Scripture: 1 Samuel 16:7b says, "For man looked on the outward appearance, but the Lord looked on the heart." So loyalty is so much more than a word—it truly reveals the heart.

The Bloodshed of Loyalty

Loyalty is driven by the matters of the heart. It is supposed to cultivate honesty, integrity, and be free of drama. But what I have experienced is just the opposite. It brought disloyalty, misplaced admiration, betrayal, distrust, and a lot of pain. Whew! And if I could mention more adjectives, I would.

As a pastor's wife laboring in the Kingdom alongside my husband, it didn't appear to me as if he was under as much turmoil as I was. Why not? What was God preparing to birth in my life? I had to learn through failures, betrayals, and misguided trust, and the lessons were undeniable training grounds, to say the least. The wounds didn't come from the outside—they came from the ones who promised to stay.

Loyalty was supposed to be my safe place in ministry. It should feel like covenant in action: unwavering, honest, protective. Instead, it unraveled into a collage of distrust, manipulation, and beautifully masked betrayal. I poured from a sacred place, but what returned felt more like performance than partnership. They professed they loved me, said they were assigned to be here with me. They cried when I prayed, shouted when I preached. They called me Mama, hugged me with holy fervor, and lingered long enough to learn my rhythms but not my heart. I watched admiration turn into entitlement. I watched proximity breed offense, and before I could blink, loyalty had grown legs and wandered into alliance with voices that never knew my sacrifice.

I feel you, sis. There's bleeding that happens when your love is real but their loyalty is situational. You feel it in your chest during altar call. You sense it when you preach but can't stop checking the room. You carry it home in silence because leaders aren't supposed to confess heartbreak— that's what they say. They're supposed to keep leading.

But one night, when the silence got too loud and the ache too deep, I stood in the sanctuary long after the benediction. And I whispered one raw, trembling question:

"Lord, how do I keep pouring when the vessel keeps leaving?"

And He answered with fire:

"You're not pouring into people. You're pouring into promise. Stay loyal to the vow—not the applause."

Whew!

That's when I learned the difference between temporary agreement and eternal covenant. True loyalty survives pruning. It stays when correction stings. It is not flattered by your gifts; it is faithful to your grit.

Oh yes, I grieved—not just their absence, but the misplaced trust that tied my soul to their potential. Because misplaced loyalty will make you bleed for people who were never assigned to carry your oil. Now, I serve differently. I still love hard, but I guard sacred space. I lay hands cautiously, but I speak boldly. I ask God to send those who won't just cheer when it's popular, but cover when it's personal.

Ministry taught me that loyalty isn't sentimental—it's spiritual. I no longer chase after people who can't honor my assignment. I serve for legacy, not likes. I lead from healing, not hurt. And for every reader who's been wounded in secret, bleeding behind the pulpit—I see you, and God sees you. And He's still writing with the ink of your tears. Let Him.

True Loyalty

True loyalty is a spiritual covenant and not a social contract. It does not hinge on convenience or applause. It is the vow made behind the veil, the whisper spoken in the wilderness of ministry, saying: I'm still called to this, even when it cuts.

For the women who stand beside the pulpit but sleep beside the prophet—for those who carry both the grace to birth vision and the grief of invisible wounds—loyalty is rarely reciprocated in equal measure. We carry the cost in quiet dignity. We smile while bleeding. We embrace while grieving. We endure while interceding.

There is a loneliness that comes from staying faithful in the face of abandonment—not just physical absence but spiritual detachment. People can still sit in pews and yet carry disconnected hearts. As First Ladies, we discern it. We feel the shift before it manifests. The conversations grow shorter, the passion grows colder, and attendance becomes inconsistent until suddenly the ones we mentored now mimic distance, and the ones we covered now question our calling. Covenant doesn't cancel itself when pressure rises.

Your Purity to Loyalty Must Remain

For those women called to stay when it feels safer to run—you are not overlooked. Heaven counts the cost. Every tear cried in silence, every prayer whispered in weariness, every seed sown in a dry season—God sees, and He knows. And He rewards the woman who remained loyal when it no longer made sense.

Loyalty looks like showing up when you're exhausted. It looks like pouring into others while your own spirit feels hollow. It looks like protecting the ministry while being pierced by its transitions. And though many won't say it, some of the greatest spiritual warriors are not on stages, but in shadows. They are the women who hold the line behind the scenes, who keep covenant even when covenant fails them.

We are those women. We are the ones who still lay hands on pillows drenched in grief, who still speak life over altars marked by absence, who still cook meals for meetings that might never produce fruit. Our reward is not in recognition—it's in revelation. Loyalty is unto God, not disconnected hearts.

The Mantle of Loyalty

The mantle of loyalty is not stitched in popularity; it is woven in suffering, sealed by obedience, and affirmed in the unseen. To carry it is to walk through fire without smelling like smoke. To bear it is to endure betrayal without losing your voice. To wear it is to serve with unwavering commitment, even when the applause has faded and the trusted have turned.

This mantle is not lightweight—it is heaven-forged. It carries the fingerprints of those who've cried in secret yet refused to quit. It rests upon the shoulders of leaders who loved deeply, led faithfully, and bled silently.

And it cannot be worn by the half-committed or the fame chasers. Only those who have been pressed in private can steward its public power.

"To whom much is given, much will be required." — Luke 12:48 (KJV)

"Be faithful unto death, and I will give you the crown of life." — Revelation 2:10 (KJV)

The mantle of loyalty is a prophetic summons in a generation allergic to staying. It invites us to return to covenant—with God, with purpose, and with people who carry assignments.

The Oil Still Flows

Loyalty may bleed, but it does not die. Though my heart has known the sting of betrayal and the silence of broken promises, I remain anchored not in people, but in purpose. Ministry taught me that loyalty is not confirmed by applause, but by endurance. It's not tested in moments of affirmation, but in seasons of absence.

So, Women of Destiny, if you've poured into those who vanished, if you've covered those who later exposed you, if you've bled in silence while leading in strength—you are not forgotten. You are chosen.

"Many are the afflictions of the righteous, but the LORD delivers him out of them all."

—Psalm 34:19 (KJV)

God never required perfection from those we serve. He asked for obedience from the ones He calls. And sometimes, obedience means standing alone in the sanctuary, holding on to covenant while everything around you changes.

Period!

This page intentionally left blank

About the Author

Dr. Kecia Reed is an empowering author, transformational leader, Apostle, Certified Life Coach, Soul Therapist, and serial entrepreneur with a passion for healing and restoration. Together with her husband, Apostle Stan Reed, she co-pastors *God's House of Refuge Ministry of Deliverance* in Suffolk, Virginia—a spiritual haven where deliverance, prophetic insight, and covenant teaching converge.

Renowned for merging academic excellence with prophetic depth, Dr. Reed equips believers to transcend emotional wounds and spiritual warfare through biblically grounded strategies. Her voice carries both wisdom and fire, guiding souls to freedom, restoration, and renewed purpose. Whether through sermons, coaching sessions, or authored works, she cultivates atmospheres where transformation is inevitable, and victory is assured.

Mercy Qualified Me: When God's Grace Calls You Beyond Your Comfort

By Lady Regina Allen

This is my story. And maybe, in some way, it's yours too.

I wish I could say I joyfully accepted the title of First Lady with grace and confidence, but the truth is, I wrestled with it. I questioned God. I questioned myself. I battled with feelings of self-doubt. I struggled with my own insecurities.

"God, are You sure about this?"

"What do I have to offer?"

"I don't have the patience to be a First Lady."

"You must have picked the wrong woman."

I didn't see myself as the polished picture of what people think a First Lady should be. I certainly never signed up for the expectations, scrutiny, and pressure that often come with the title.

I watched other First Ladies from afar—graceful, confident, poised, and put together. I admired them. I respected them. But I never saw myself as one of them. Me? With all my flaws? With my quiet struggles? With my imperfect past and insecurities? That couldn't be me.

But then life, love, and God happened.

I fell in love with a man who was after God's own heart. He wasn't a Bishop or a Pastor when I met him. He was a humble, grounded man with a growing anointing, a servant's heart, a deep love for people, and a genuine passion to build the Kingdom of God. I watched him grow in grace and stature—not just in title, but in wisdom, in compassion, and in leadership. I stood by his side through each chapter: as he became a Pastor, then a District Elder, and now a Suffragan Bishop. Yet with each elevation he received, I still sometimes felt unqualified for the position God was calling me to stand in beside him.

There was a season—maybe like the one you've had or are in—when I looked up and quietly inquired, my lips shaking as tears ran down my cheeks, "Lord, did You make a mistake?" But each time I asked that question, I sensed the Lord responding, not with condemnation, but with gentle reassurance:

"I make no mistakes. I chose you on purpose."

He accepted the call to pastor, and I was expected to step into a new calling too.

Then one day, his calling met my fears.

God doesn't call the qualified. He qualifies the call.

I had to learn that my insecurities didn't disqualify me; they made room for His strength to be made perfect in my weakness (2 Corinthians 12:9). I had to understand that my background, personality, and pain weren't obstacles—they were instruments God could use for His glory.

Accepting the Assignment

There came a moment when I had to stop wrestling and start accepting. Accepting the call didn't mean I had all the answers. It didn't mean I had overcome every fear. It meant that I said yes anyway.

Saying yes means recognizing that this role is not just tied to your husband's ministry, but also part of God's divine purpose for your life. You are chosen to walk beside, uplift, and spiritually support a man of God, and to be a visible, godly presence in the church and community.

Accepting the role of First Lady wasn't about becoming someone else; it was about becoming more of who God always intended me to be.

And with that yes came transformation.

I realized that my purpose wasn't just to sit pretty or show up when the camera was on. My calling as a First Lady was to serve, to nurture, to intercede, to mentor, to protect, and to walk boldly and authentically as a woman of God.

Learning to Walk in My Own Shoes

One of the greatest lessons I learned on this journey is that you don't have to fit anyone else's shoes to walk in your calling.

Early on, I searched for First Ladies to mentor me. I encountered many different styles of First Ladies, but none at the time felt like a reflection of who I was called to be.

With love in his voice, my husband said, "Honey, be who God made you to be. You don't have to fit into anyone else's shoes as a First Lady."

And the Holy Spirit also reminded me:

"I didn't call you to be her. I called you to be you."

There's freedom in that. When I stopped comparing, my authenticity became my ministry. People connected with my honesty, not my perfection. Women didn't need another untouchable role model; they needed a real woman who had been through the fire and still stood with faith.

Finding Strength in God

Saying yes to the call doesn't mean it stops being hard. There are still days I feel overlooked, misunderstood, or stretched too thin. There are times I feel like I'm bleeding while leading, pouring out while privately dealing with my own struggles, and not being replenished.

But I've learned to find strength in the secret place.

The more time I spend with God in prayer, in worship, and in His Word, the more I'm reminded that I'm not alone. Everything I put out in public is quietly restored in the secret place. His presence comforts me.

He sees the tears I cry that no one else sees. He hears the prayers I whisper in the quiet. He feels every burden I carry, and He sustains me through it all.

Managing the Weight of the Unexpected

I won't pretend the journey got easy overnight. While I accepted the call, there were still days I battled the weight of the role—the opinions, the isolation, the assumptions, and the pressure to always "have it together" stress me at times.

But what carried me was not my strength—it was the mercy of God, made new every morning.

I've learned that we cannot carry the mantle without also carrying the mission. And we cannot carry the mission without depending entirely on His mercy. The mantle does not come because of our greatness; it comes because of His grace.

Here's what I discovered during my lowest moments as a First Lady:

Mercy covered me when I wanted to quit.

Mercy empowered me when I didn't feel capable.

Mercy reminded me that I didn't have to be perfect; I just had to be present.

Many women want the ministry but not the weight that comes with it.

I didn't ask for the weight either, but I've come to see it as sacred. When you carry something sacred, it must be handled with humility, and mercy makes humility possible.

I realized the calling wasn't about being "seen"; it was about being submitted to God, to the mission, to the process, and to the people.

Mercy Met Me Before the Title Did

Before I was ever called "First Lady," I was just me—flawed, learning, and still a work in progress. Truthfully, that hasn't changed. I'm still being transformed daily by the mercy of God.

When I asked if He made a mistake, I was really struggling to believe His mercy could cover my fears, failures, and inexperience. I thought God made decisions based on perfection—but I learned He works through purpose.

It was mercy that called Moses despite his speech issue.

Mercy that chose David despite his sins.

Mercy that restored Peter after his denial.

And mercy that looked at me—not the polished version, but the real me—and said, "Yes, her."

The beauty of mercy is that it qualifies us even when we feel unqualified. Mercy doesn't just forgive our past; it redeems it, using every piece to build something useful for the Kingdom. I came to see that God wasn't asking me to become someone else to carry the mantle of First Lady. He was asking me to become more of who He created me to be—through His mercy.

His mercy is the foundation beneath every decision and every step. The role is demanding, but His compassion renews me daily.

We don't walk this journey alone. Mercy meets us in our weakness, gives us grace for our imperfections, and strength when doubt creeps in. Through it, we grow, serve, and reflect Christ—not through perfection, but through His perfect love.

Conclusion

As I look back over my life—the unexpected turns, the unanswered questions, the unspoken fears—I can say with confidence that God didn't make a mistake. He made a miracle out of a woman who felt unworthy.

The title "First Lady" may have caught me by surprise, but it never surprised God. He knew what He was doing when He called me. He knew my flaws. He knew my fears. And still, He whispered, "You are Mine, and this is your assignment."

That's mercy.

Not the kind that just forgives, but the kind that transforms.

So, if you're standing at the edge of your call, unsure whether to step forward, remember this:

You are not here by accident.

You were not called by mistake.

You are not expected to be perfect.

You are chosen, loved, equipped, and covered by the mercy of God.

Your past didn't cancel your purpose. Your doubts didn't destroy your destiny. His mercy is greater than your history and more powerful than your fear.

So, wear the mantle—not with pride, but with purpose.

Lead—not with performance, but with passion.

Serve—not from obligation, but from overflow.

Because when God extends mercy, it's never a mistake.

I give honor to my wonderful husband, Suffragan Bishop David Allen, Jr. He has always encouraged me, even when I couldn't encourage myself. His consistent belief in who I am—not just as his wife, but as a woman of God—has carried me. When I doubted myself, he reminded me of God's choice. When I tried to hide in the shadows, he lovingly pulled me forward. His support has been a steady voice echoing the truth of heaven in moments when I struggled to hear it on my own.

In ministry, my husband and I have learned the rhythm of grace and partnership. When I am strong, I push him forward, and when he is strong, he pushes me. It's not about competition, but divine collaboration. God has woven our strengths and weaknesses together to create a balance that only He could orchestrate. There are days when the weight of the call feels heavy on him, and I become the voice of encouragement, the intercessor, and the gentle nudge that reminds him he's not alone. And then there are days when I grow weary, uncertain, or overwhelmed, and he becomes my strength—covering me in prayer, reminding me of my purpose, and pushing me gently back into position.

This mutual pushing isn't pressure; it's partnership, fueled by love, strengthened by mercy, and grounded in our shared call. Together, we walk in the truth that God didn't just call one of us—He called **us**.

About the Author

Lady Regina Allen is an outgoing, faith-filled woman known for her warmth, energy, and genuine love for people. She has been a devoted member of Christ Temple Apostolic Church for over forty-seven years and has faithfully served in leadership alongside her husband, Bishop David Allen, Jr., for the past fifteen years.

Throughout her many years of service at CTAC, Lady Regina has ministered in a variety of capacities, including Hospitality, Outreach, Kid's Church, Administration, and Office Management. She also serves as the Director and President of the Victorious Women's Ministry, where she encourages and equips women to grow in faith and purpose.

In addition to her local church leadership, Lady Regina serves as President of the Texas State Ministers' Wives and Widows Auxiliary under the Texas State Council of the Pentecostal Assemblies of the World (PAW).

Her life and ministry are anchored in Jeremiah 29:11, as she continues to trust God's perfect plan and faithfully serve His people.

NEVER GIVE UP

By Apostle Sharon Motley

JUST WALK AWAY

"I'm DONE. I QUIT. I CAN'T do this ANYMORE."

I can't tell you how many times those words have rung out in my mind and come through my mouth. Frustration overwhelmed me like a tsunami overtaking a city. Questions surfaced: *Why me, Lord? What did I do to deserve this? How much longer will I have to endure this trauma? How is this even fair?*

I had given my life to people who took it in their hands and smashed it like an unwanted gnat. Members who said they "had my back," only for me to look around and see the knife they held—turning it, creating devastation.

I remember thinking: *I didn't sign up for this.* I had a good job as a Registered Nurse—eight hours and go home. My life was mine and belonged to no one else. But there I was: ministry 24/7, like a bad dream that never seemed to end.

Becoming weary at the day-in and day-out travesty of ministry, knowing it shouldn't be this way—but here I am, as if caught in an alligator's death roll. No way out. Death seemed certain—and indeed that in itself might be the blessing, at least there would be an end.

But then I remembered the scripture:

Galatians 6:9:

"Let us not become weary in doing good, for at the proper time we will reap a harvest if we do not give up."

To be honest, I wasn't looking for a harvest. I was simply seeking peace—and maybe a little splash of joy.

ANOTHER JOB PLEASE

As a First Lady, we face many challenges. We experience the good, the bad, and many times the ugly.

Though I wouldn't change my life as a First Lady, there are times I shake my head and guard my heart from the pain that has been inflicted upon me. I have had to hold my head up after those who called me pastor, friend, sister, and co-laborer walked away.

And not just walked away—but tried to destroy me as they went.

The stress and strain at times can be almost unbearable. The heartbreak of people leaving feels as if someone has died, and the funeral never seems to end. Tears flow like an endless river.

There are moments when you simply want to crawl into bed and sleep for a long season—or maybe get in the car and drive until the gas tank runs empty.

I tell you all of this to say: we have been there and we have the t-shirt to prove it.

But we are still here.

We are still moving.

We are still ministering.

We didn't give up.

And we are here to tell you—**YOU CAN TOO!**

God will turn your pain into purpose, your hurt into help, and your test into a testimony.

REWARDED FOR THIS?

In 1941, Winston Churchill spoke to Harrow College and delivered a famous line that has echoed around the world:

"Never yield to force; never yield to the apparently overwhelming might of the enemy... Never give in, never give in, never, never, never, never—in nothing, great or small, large or petty—never give in except to convictions of honour and good sense."

His message of never giving up was heard across the world. Though he spoke in the natural, it rang loudly in the spirit.

Giving up is not something new. It is a force people have fought against for ages. We are not the first to face it, and we certainly won't be the last.

I love the scripture found in:

2 Chronicles 15:7

"But as for you, be strong and do not give up, for your work will be rewarded."

I treasure the last part of that verse: your work will be rewarded.

Sometimes we feel as though we are spinning our wheels—taking ten steps forward and twenty steps back. I once heard someone say:

"I would love ministry if it weren't for people."

Working with people can be difficult. Personalities, conflict, rejection, and betrayal can cut straight to the core.

I recall a young woman in our church whom I poured into. I bought clothes for her and her child. I allowed her to travel with me. I even paid bills for her.

She was a good person—and honestly, she still is.

But somewhere in the middle of my kindness, she decided she wanted to be me.

Satan deceived her into believing she could take my position. Familiarity set in, and she began to disrespect me on many levels.

The hurt was great.

The pain was almost unbearable.

She apologized.

She cried.

She repented.

But the very next week, the behavior started again.

No one would have ever imagined this girl doing such things.

I kept my mouth closed to others, but I called her and her husband in and dismissed them from the church.

It was difficult—but necessary.

For my peace and my sanity.

If I see her today, I will speak. But the boat of a forever friendship sailed long ago.

During that season I wanted to quit. I wanted to let go, walk away, and lie in bed forever.

But I couldn't.

There was a calling on my life.

The calling on your husband's life does not mean you are not called, gifted, and anointed.

God has a plan and purpose for you.

1 Corinthians 11:1 says:

"Follow me, as I follow Christ."

God has called you to lead people into His kingdom.

Never settle for the lie that you are less valuable.

If you don't know your value, the enemy will convince you to give up.

You must keep your eyes fixed on the Word of God.

STANDING IN THE GAP

Reflecting on the scripture that says your work will be rewarded, God will also use you in your marriage to stand in the gap for your husband.

The suicide rate and depression among pastors are a growing concern. Pastors report high levels of stress, isolation, and emotional exhaustion. A significant number cite overwhelming stress as a primary reason they consider leaving ministry.

As wives and partners in ministry, we are there to stand in the gap—to encourage, love, and speak life into our husbands.

Over the years I have observed that many pastors struggle with insecurity. When people leave the church, it can intensify those feelings and cause them to question their value.

That is where we come in.

God strengthens us to support them—to encourage them and speak life into them.

Sometimes our assignment is to help prevent them from giving up.

God will help you as you help them.

BLINDED BY MINISTRY

I remember a season when my husband was so consumed with ministry that he looked right past me. He ignored my pain and my cries for help.

With no one to talk to, I sat in an ocean of loneliness.

During that time, I cried myself to sleep many nights, wishing the pain would end.

But in the midst of the storm, I ran to the Rock of my salvation.

Psalm 56:3-4 (ESV)

"When I am afraid, I put my trust in you. In God, whose word I praise—in God I trust; I shall not be afraid. What can flesh do to me?"

I threw myself into prayer and into the Word.

I made up my mind that I was going to fulfill God's plan for my life.

I developed laser focus. My commitment to the Father became my obsession.

I refused to look to the north, south, east, or west.

I decided that if God was going to use anyone—it was going to be me.

I would be the best wife.

The greatest mother.

And then something miraculous happened.

God turned my husband's heart.

When I gave everything to God, He restored my marriage. My husband became my closest friend.

He saw me again.

What changed?

I made God my priority—not people, not my husband, not my children.

Only Him.

When I surrendered fully to God and His plan, my heart settled into one conviction:

Giving up is not an option.

Friend, purpose in your heart today—**never give up.**

CLOSING

One of the greatest things you can do in life and ministry is to fix your heart and mind on the Father.

Have a made-up mind that says:

"I will never give up."

I will continue doing what God has called me to do.

I will not be moved.

I will not lose focus.

Isaiah 26:3 (KJV)

"Thou wilt keep him in perfect peace, whose mind is stayed on thee: because he trusteth in thee."

So today—and every day—look unto Jesus.

Keep your eyes on Him.

He will sustain you in all that you do.

And friend—

NEVER, NEVER, NEVER… GIVE UP.

About the Author

Apostle Sharon Motley has been in fulltime ministry for 40 years, where she serves alongside her husband, Apostle Bill Motley. Known for her bold and unapologetic style, Apostle Sharon delivers the uncompromised Word of Faith with clarity and authority. As she speaks truth into the lives of others, hearts are opened, chains are broken, and captives are set free by the power of God. Through her own powerful testimony of healing, many have found hope and the anointing to be released from their past. She ministers with a strong deliverance anointing and flows freely in the Gifts of the Spirit, with a distinct prophetic grace. A passionate voice for the nations, Apostle Sharon has traveled extensively, witnessing miracles, healings, and deliverance across multiple countries. She has a heart for the mission field and a deep commitment to global ministry.

Together with her husband, she serves as president of **Kingdom Ministerial Affiliation (KMA)**, an organization dedicated to equipping and empowering pastors and ministers for effective kingdom work.

Apostle Sharon is the author of several powerful resources, including *30 Days of Healing devotional, 31 Days of Healing, The Healing Word* (book and CD)*, and Hymns for Him* (music CD). She is also the co-author of *From Breakdown to Breakthrough and More Than a First Lady.*

She is the devoted wife of Apostle Bill Motley for the past 41 ye and the proud mother of four beautiful children.

Obedience to God: It's A Priority

By Dr. Doris Loftin

Obedience in the Hierarchy of Life

As we travel through this temporary earthly existence, we often face conflicting thoughts and sometimes conflicting truths or facts about what is right and wrong. Scientists, psychologists, psychiatrists, and even some Christian counselors may respond with a challenge to analyze situations, circumstances, or relationships and to do "what you think is best for you."

In this twenty-first century, people are encouraged to be independent, confident, self-assured, assertive, self-reliant, motivated, and financially focused. These are positive attributes, but we must be careful as to where we place these attributes in our priorities or hierarchy of life.

Life operates within a hierarchy of values. Our priorities determine our choices, shape our character, and ultimately define our destiny. For many people, success, wealth, or influence occupy the highest place. For others, relationships, comfort, or personal freedom take precedence. Yet for the believer, obedience to God must stand at the pinnacle of this hierarchy. It is the compass that aligns every other pursuit under God's divine order.

Jesus said clearly in John 14:15, "If you love Me, keep My commandments." Love for God is not proved by emotion, but by obedience. Our devotion is measured not by how we feel about God, but by how faithfully we follow His Word. When obedience occupies its rightful place above ambition, comfort, and convenience, the believer begins to walk in harmony with God's perfect will.

The Bible repeatedly ties obedience to love, blessing, and spiritual maturity. Moses told Israel, "If you fully obey the Lord your God and carefully follow all His commands... the Lord your God will set you high above all the nations on earth" (Deuteronomy 28:1). True greatness, therefore, is not achieved by power or position, but by submission and by choosing to do what God says, when He says it, and how He says it.

We make choices every day, all day. Do we place obedience to God in a high place as we are making decisions in our daily lives: when we are relating to family, friends, co-workers, and strangers; when we are making big and small decisions; and when we are working in the church and the community?

Obedience in Daily Living

Obedience begins in the ordinary. The measure of our faith is not just in grand moments of sacrifice, but in the quiet, consistent choices of everyday life. Jesus said, "Blessed rather are those who hear the word of God and obey it" (Luke 11:28).

Daily obedience may look like honesty in business, integrity in speech, faithfulness in small duties, or patience in trials. It is in these moments that God shapes our hearts. Each act of obedience, no matter how small, becomes a steppingstone toward spiritual maturity.

James warns, "Do not merely listen to the word, and so deceive yourselves. Do what it says" (James 1:22). The Word of God is not meant only for information but for transformation. A life that hears yet does not act is a life built on sand. But when obedience becomes our daily habit, God's truth finds expression through our actions, and His blessings follow naturally.

In daily living, it is important to be constant in prayer and to ask God for guidance in our daily walk. Living daily according to the Word should be the goal of every follower of Christ. The "new creation" that we have become is exemplified to those who are still seeking by our daily lives. Preach your sermon by your daily walk.

Obedience in daily living also protects us. Each time we choose to align with God's will, we guard our hearts from sin's deception. Every obedient step is a declaration that God's way is wiser than ours.

Obedience in Relationships with Others

Obedience to God inevitably shapes how we treat others. Love, forgiveness, humility, and service are not optional virtues; they are divine commands. When we obey God in our relationships, we reflect His nature to those around us. Our first priority in relationships should be with our own household, our families, and our loved ones, and then to others.

Jesus summarized the law in two commands: love God and love your neighbor. Obedience to these commands restores broken relationships, bridges divisions, and promotes peace. It requires humility to forgive when wronged, to serve when it is inconvenient, and to speak truth when it is uncomfortable.

In our families, obedience to God means honoring parents, nurturing our spouses, and raising children with godly principles. In the workplace, it means integrity, diligence, and respect for authority. In friendships, it means loyalty and honesty. These acts of relational obedience demonstrate to others that God's Word governs our hearts, not emotions or circumstances.

As John 14:21 says, "Whoever has My commands and keeps them is the one who loves Me. The one who loves Me will be loved by My Father, and I too will love them and show Myself to them." The reward of relational obedience is divine fellowship. God reveals Himself in deeper ways to those who walk in His love.

Obedience in Decision Making

Life is filled with decisions—some small, others life-changing. Each decision tests whether our trust truly rests in God's wisdom or in our own understanding. Obedience in decision making means surrendering our will to God's direction, even when His way seems uncertain or difficult.

Obedience doesn't always make sense to human logic. Abraham left his homeland not knowing where he was going. Peter cast his net again after a night of failure simply because Jesus said to. Mary accepted the divine call despite public shame. Each act of obedience unlocked a miracle.

When we submit our decisions to God through prayer, His Word, and the leading of the Holy Spirit, He guides us toward His best. Proverbs 3:5–6 reminds us, "Trust in the Lord with all your heart and lean not on your own understanding; in all your ways submit to Him, and He will make your paths straight."

Obedience in decision making is not passive; it is active trust that believes God knows better than we do. It requires faith to wait, courage to act, and humility to yield. Every time we obey His prompting, we grow in discernment and experience His faithfulness afresh.

Obedience in Kingdom Work

Serving in God's Kingdom demands more than enthusiasm; it demands obedience. Kingdom work succeeds not by human ability but by divine direction. Jesus' ministry was marked by perfect obedience to the Father: "I do nothing on My own but speak just what the Father has taught Me" (John 8:28).

When believers obey God's instructions in ministry—whether preaching, teaching, giving, or serving—they align with heaven's agenda.

Disobedience can hinder God's purposes. King Saul learned this painfully when he spared what God had commanded to destroy. Samuel rebuked him, saying, "To obey is better than sacrifice" (1 Samuel 15:22).

In Kingdom service, obedience often requires stepping out of comfort zones, trusting God for provision, and persevering despite opposition. Yet each act of faithful obedience multiplies eternal impact. The church grows, lives are transformed, and the name of Jesus is glorified when God's servants simply do what He says.

Obedience to God Brings Blessings from God

God's blessings are intricately tied to obedience. Deuteronomy 28:1 declares that if we fully obey the Lord, "all these blessings will come upon you and accompany you." These blessings include favor, protection, fruitfulness, and spiritual authority.

Obedience opens the door to God's promises because it demonstrates trust. God delights in blessing His obedient children because it positions us to receive what His love desires to give.

However, obedience must be motivated by love, not greed. Jesus said in John 14:15, "If you love Me, keep My commandments." True obedience flows from a heart that loves God and desires His presence more than His gifts. When love motivates obedience, blessings naturally follow—not just material blessings, but peace, joy, and a close relationship with God.

The greatest blessing of obedience is not prosperity, but presence—the nearness of God Himself. When we walk in obedience, we walk with Him, and that walk with God is the highest reward.

Conclusion: The Call to Obedient Living

Obedience is not an outdated virtue. Obedience is the expression of genuine faith. It defines our love for God, shapes our character, and unlocks divine favor. Every area of life—our habits, relationships, decisions, and service—finds order and blessing when submitted to God's authority.

To obey is to trust that God's way is the best way. It is to choose submission over self-will, faith over fear, and love over convenience. The obedient life is not always the easiest, but it is always the most rewarding.

As we align our lives under God's Word, may our prayer echo the words of Samuel:

"Speak, Lord, for Your servant is listening."

For the one who listens and obeys will surely experience the fullness of God's blessing.

This page intentionally left blank

140

About the Author

Dr. Doris Loftin is a graduate of Morgan State University and the University of Maryland School of Social Work, and has earned a Doctorate of Humane Letters from the Eastern Theological Seminary and College.

Dr. Loftin is a clinical social worker who has served in public social services agencies , as an instructor at the Community College of Baltimore, adjunct professor for the University of Maryland School of Social Work and Morgan State University, and in private practice.

Dr. Loftin serves actively with the Greater Baltimore Ministers' Wives and Ministers' Widows Fellowship, Maryland Association of Ministers' Wives and Ministers' Widows, International Association of Ministers' Wives and Ministers' Widows, and the Women's Auxiliary of the United Baptist Missionary Convention of Maryland, Inc.

Rev. Dr. Doris Loftin is a licensed and ordained minister of the gospel, teacher, counselor, workshop facilitator, and Leading Lady Emeritus of the Pleasant Rock Baptist Church, Baltimore, Maryland, where her husband of 60 years, Bishop Timothy Loftin, is founder and Pastor Emeritus.

Lady Loftin and her husband are the proud parents of three children and six grandchildren.

"I press toward the mark for the prize of the high calling of God in Christ Jesus." Philippians 3:14

Push Past the Pain

By Pastor Jacqueline Renee Duncan

There are moments in life that split your story in two—the life you knew before, and the life you never imagined you'd have to live. For me, that moment came the day, my husband Phillip G. Duncan who had a major stroke on September 7, 2014.

My husband had always been the definition of strength. Twenty two years in the Marine Corps had carved discipline into his bones. A black belt in karate, he had stood on a mat in Japan and earned third place on an international stage in Japan. He was the man people looked at and thought, *unshakeable.* And for years, I believed that too.

But when the stroke hit, all that strength—his power, his precision, his presence—seemed to slip through my fingers. I felt unprotected in a way I had never known. Watching a man who had once commanded rooms now struggle to command his own body was a pain I didn't have language for. It wasn't just his loss; it was ours.

And yet, life didn't pause to let me grieve the change.

"Grief moves through you like a tide—retreating, returning, reshaping the shoreline of who you are."

While caring for Phillip and our daughter, I stepped into his role as Pastor, carrying a mantle I never expected to wear. I worked long hours on my job to keep our home and our church from slipping away. Every day felt like a battlefield of its own—one where the enemy wasn't a person, but exhaustion, fear, and the weight of responsibility.

But even in the heaviness, something in me refused to break. I learned to push past the pain—not because I was fearless, but because love demanded it, purpose required it, and God strengthened me for it.

This chapter is about that push. The push that hurts. The push that stretches you. The push that reveals who you are when life strips everything else away.

But life didn't pause to let me process that pain.

"You are learning to breathe in a world that changed without asking you first."

While Phillip recovered, the responsibilities he once carried fell onto my shoulders. I stepped into his role as Pastor—not because I felt ready, but because the church needed leadership, and our church needed stability. I worked long hours on my job to keep the bills paid, the lights on, and the roof over our heads. I cared for Phillip, cared for our daughter, and tried to hold together a life that felt like it was unraveling thread by thread.

There were nights I cried quietly so no one would hear. Nights when exhaustion pressed so heavily on my chest that I wondered how I would get up the next morning. Nights when I questioned God, not out of disbelief, but out of desperation: *Lord, how do I carry all of this? How do I stay strong when everything hurts?*

But even in the heaviness, something in me refused to break. I didn't feel strong, but strength showed up anyway—in small ways, in quiet ways, in ways I didn't recognize until much later. Strength showed up in the mornings I didn't want to get out of bed but did. In the sermons I preached even when my heart was trembling. In the bills I paid when the numbers didn't add up. In the prayers I whispered when I didn't have words left.

I learned that pushing past the pain doesn't mean ignoring it. It means moving *with* it. It means trusting that God can carry what you can't. It means believing that purpose can still rise out of seasons that feel like loss.

"Some sorrows settle in the bones, not to break you, but to remind you that you have depth."

Phillip's stroke changed our lives, but it also revealed something I had never fully seen in myself: the strength God had planted in me long before I ever needed it. A strength that wasn't loud or forceful, but steady. A strength that didn't replace Phillip's, but complemented it. A strength that allowed me to lead, to protect, to provide, and to love in ways I never imagined I could.

This chapter of my life taught me that pain doesn't disqualify you from purpose. Sometimes, it's the very thing that pushes you into it.

And so I kept going. Not because I was fearless, but because I was called. Not because I was unhurt, but because I was determined. Not because the journey was easy, but because giving up was never an option.

This is what it means to push past the pain: to keep moving when your heart is heavy, to keep believing when your world shifts, and to keep standing even when your knees tremble.

And by God's grace, I did.

"You carry storms inside you, yet there is something in you that keeps reaching for the horizon."

Phillip could not walk or talk clearly and he was in rehab for six weeks learning how to live his life again it was painful for me to see and for his daughter Shekinah to see, Our spiritual parents stepped up to help in ways I couldn't.

The hospital became our second home before I even realized it. Those first days were a blur of machines beeping, nurses moving in and out, and doctors speaking in a language that felt too heavy to understand. But the hardest part wasn't the medical terms or the uncertainty. It was seeing Phillip—my strong, disciplined, unstoppable husband—lying in a bed unable to walk, unable to talk clearly, unable to be the man he had always been.

His words came out slow, tangled, fighting their way through a body that no longer obeyed him. His steps—when he could take them—were shaky and unsure. And every time he tried to move, I could see the frustration in his eyes. This was a man who had marched in formation, fought through training, competed internationally, and led a congregation with authority. Now he had to relearn how to lift a fork, how to form a sentence, how to stand without falling.

It broke something inside me every single day.

And it broke something inside our daughter, Shekinah, too. She was still young, still forming her understanding of the world, and suddenly her hero—her daddy—was different. I watched her try to be brave, try to smile, try to pretend she wasn't scared. But children feel things deeply, even when they don't have the words. She would sit by his bedside, holding his hand, looking at him with eyes full of questions she didn't know how to ask.

There were moments when I had to step out of the room just to breathe. Moments when the weight of watching them both hurt felt like too much. Moments when I wondered how much more my heart could take.

But even in that valley, God sent help.

"There are moments when the world moves on without me, and I stand still, holding the pieces of what used to be."

Our church family, In His Presence, stepped up in ways I couldn't have imagined. They prayed. Some visited. They brought meals. They covered responsibilities I didn't have the strength or time to handle. They stood in the gap—not just for Phillip, but for me. For us. They became hands that lifted, voices that encouraged, and shoulders that steadied me when I felt like collapsing.

"I'm not trying to be brave; I'm just trying to make it through the day without collapsing inside myself."

And then came rehab.

Six weeks of watching Phillip fight for every inch of progress. Six weeks of therapy sessions that pushed him physically, mentally, and emotionally. Six weeks of victories that looked small to the world but felt monumental to us—lifting his leg, forming a clear word, taking a step without assistance. Six weeks of setbacks that reminded us how fragile recovery could be.

I sat through sessions where he tried to speak and the words wouldn't come. I watched him try to move his arm and it refused. I saw the frustration, the anger, the sadness. And I felt every bit of it with him.

But I also saw something else.

I saw determination. I saw courage. I saw the Marine in him rise up, even when his body was weak. I saw a man who refused to quit, even when quitting would have been easier. And I saw God strengthening him in ways that didn't look like the strength he once had, but were just as powerful.

Rehab wasn't just teaching Phillip how to live again. It was teaching us how to live again—differently, painfully, but still together.

"You are not the ruins; you are the one walking through them, gathering pieces of yourself as you go."

And through it all, I kept pushing past the pain. Not because I didn't feel it, but because my love for him demanded it. Because my family needed me. Because my calling required it. Because God sustained me.

There came a moment—one I didn't see coming—when everything I had been holding inside finally caught up with me. I had been moving on autopilot for weeks: hospital visits, rehab sessions, working a long hour job, preaching on Sundays, caring for Shekinah, managing the house, and trying to be strong for Phillip when he needed strength the most. I kept telling myself, *Just keep going. Just keep pushing.* But even the strongest push has a limit.

My breaking point came one evening after a long day at the rehab center. Phillip had struggled through his speech therapy session, and I could see the frustration building in him. He tried to say a simple sentence, and the words tangled together. He slammed his hand against the armrest— not out of anger at me, but out of anger at his own body. I reached for him, but he pulled away, tears filling his eyes. That was the moment I realized how deeply he was hurting, not just physically but emotionally. The Marine in him, the fighter in him, the protector in him—he felt like all of that had been stripped away.

Shekinah saw it too. She saw how weak and fragile her Daddy was, her little face looked confused and scared when she would see him. I wanted to comfort both of them but I felt like I was drowning myself.

One night, after I put Shekinah to bed and after I had called Phillip at the rehab, I went into the bathroom, closed the door, and slid down to the floor. And I cried. Not the quiet tears I had been holding back for weeks. This was a deep, shaking, uncontrollable cry—the kind that comes from a place you didn't even know existed. I cried for Phillip. I cried for Shekinah. I cried for the life we had lost. I cried for the weight I was carrying. I cried because I didn't know how much longer I could keep going.

I felt empty. I felt alone. I felt like I had failed everyone who needed me.

But in that moment of complete brokenness, something happened. Not suddenly, not dramatically, but quietly—like a whisper settling into the room.

It was as if God met me right there on that bathroom floor.

Not with answers. Not with explanations. But with presence.

A stillness came over me, and I felt a strength that wasn't mine. A reminder that I didn't have to carry everything by myself. A reassurance that even when I felt invisible, overwhelmed, and undone, God saw me. God was holding me. God was sustaining me.

That was my breakthrough.

"Even in the quiet collapse inside you, something small and stubborn keeps choosing the light."

Not because the situation changed overnight. Not because Phillip suddenly recovered. Not because the responsibilities disappeared. But because I changed. Something in me shifted. I realized that pushing past the pain didn't mean pretending I wasn't hurting. It meant trusting that God could use my pain to produce something deeper in me—resilience, compassion, endurance, and a strength I didn't know I had.

"Your tears are not weakness; they are the language of a soul refusing to go numb."

From that moment on, I stopped trying to be superhuman. I allowed myself to feel. I allowed myself to ask for help. I allowed myself to lean on the people God had placed around me. And I allowed God to carry the weight I had been trying to lift alone.

My breakthrough wasn't loud. It wasn't dramatic. It was a quiet surrender. A moment where I finally said, *Lord, I can't do this without You.* And He answered, *You don't have to.*

That night didn't erase the pain, but it gave me the strength to keep moving through it. It reminded me that breaking doesn't mean you're weak. Sometimes breaking is the only way God can rebuild you stronger.

And from that point forward, I pushed past the pain—not in my own power, but in His.

"Some nights your soul feels like a cracked lantern, but even then, a little light escapes through the fractures."

Balancing a job, caregiving, and pastoring wasn't something I planned for. It wasn't something I trained for. It was something life handed me without warning, and I had no choice but to rise to it. Every day felt like a marathon I hadn't signed up for, but somehow still had to finish.

My mornings started before the sun. I would get up, call and check on Phillip, make sure he was okay, and then get Shekinah ready for school. I tried to keep her routine as normal as possible, even though nothing about our life felt normal anymore. I wanted her to feel safe, even when I didn't feel safe myself anymore.

After dropping her off, I went straight to my job. I worked with a heaviness in my chest, always wondering how Phillip was doing, always praying he was okay. When my shift ended, I rushed to the rehab center in Laurel MD to sit with him during therapy. I wanted him to know he wasn't fighting alone. I wanted him to feel my presence, even when I couldn't take away his pain.

Then came job number two which was ministry, I worked evenings, pushing through exhaustion because the bills didn't care that my husband had a stroke. The mortgage didn't care. The church lights didn't care. Life kept moving, and I had to move with it.

And in the middle of all of that, I was still the Pastor.

I preached on Sundays with a heart that was both broken and burning. I stood before the congregation carrying my own pain while trying to pour hope into others. There were Sundays when I felt empty, when I wondered what I could possibly give. But every time I stepped into that pulpit, God met me there. He filled the places where I had nothing left. He spoke through me even when I felt voiceless. He strengthened me even when my knees were trembling.

Pastoring during that season wasn't about perfection. It was about presence. It was about showing up, even when I was hurting. It was about letting the church see that faith doesn't make you immune to struggle—it carries you through it.

Caregiving was its own ministry. Helping Phillip dress. Helping him eat. Helping him walk. Helping him speak. Helping him rediscover pieces of himself that the stroke tried to steal. Some days he was hopeful. Some days he was frustrated. Some days he was quiet. And I had to learn how to love him through all of it.

There were nights when I came home from work, checked on him, checked on Shekinah, and then sat in the dark living room because I didn't have the energy to turn on the lights. Nights when my body was tired, my mind was tired, and my spirit felt stretched thin. Nights when I wondered how long I could keep going like this.

But somehow, I did.

Not because I was superwoman. Not because I had it all together. Not because I never felt overwhelmed. I kept going because God carried me. Because purpose pushed me. Because love anchored me. Because quitting was never an option.

"Your pain is a silent river, carving new paths through you, reshaping the landscape without asking permission."

Balancing my new life, caregiving, and pastoring didn't make me perfect—it made me stronger. It taught me how to lean on God in ways I never had before. It taught me how to ask for help. It taught me how to rest in moments, even if the rest was only five minutes in the car before walking into the next responsibility.

It taught me that strength isn't loud. Sometimes strength is quiet. Sometimes strength is simply showing up again and again, even when everything in you wants to collapse.

And through it all, I learned that God doesn't just give strength—He is strength. He became the thread that held my life together when everything else felt like it was unraveling.

Even in the hardest seasons, God has a way of slipping hope into the cracks—quietly, gently, almost like a whisper reminding you that the story isn't over. Phillip's recovery was full of painful days, but it was also full of small miracles that kept us going.

One of the first moments of hope came during a physical therapy session. Phillip had been struggling for days to lift his leg without assistance. Every attempt left him frustrated, exhausted, and silent in a way that broke my heart. But one afternoon, as the therapist encouraged him to try again, something shifted. His leg moved—just an inch, maybe two—but it moved. And the look on his face… it was the first spark I had seen in him since the stroke.

I clapped. The therapist clapped. Even Phillip let out a small laugh, surprised by his own progress. It wasn't a big step to the world, but to us, it felt like he had climbed a mountain. That tiny movement reminded me that healing doesn't always come in leaps. Sometimes it comes in inches.

Another moment came during speech therapy. For weeks, his words were tangled, slow, and hard to understand. He would try to speak, and the frustration would rise in him like a wave. But one day, as Shekinah sat beside him, he looked at her and said her name—clear, steady, and unmistakable.

"She…ki…nah."

She froze. Then her eyes filled with tears, and she threw her arms around him. I stood there watching them, my own tears falling before I could stop them. Hearing him say her name again was like hearing a piece of our life return. After the stroke Phillip would always call her Jernice which was his sister's name. It was a reminder that the man we loved was still there, still fighting, still pushing.

There were other moments too—quiet ones that didn't make noise but made a difference.

The day he stood without the therapist holding him.

The day he fed himself without dropping the spoon.

The day he remembered a scripture and whispered it under his breath.

The day he smiled at me—not the tired smile he had been giving, but the real one, the one that reached his eyes.

"Pain may shape you, but it doesn't get to decide who you become."

Each moment was a thread of hope, weaving itself into the fabric of our new reality. They didn't erase the pain, but they softened it. They didn't undo the struggle, but they reminded us that progress was happening, even when it felt slow.

And then there was the moment that changed everything for me.

Phillip was practicing walking with the parallel bars. His steps were shaky, uneven, and slow. I stood at the end of the bars, cheering him on quietly, trying not to overwhelm him. He took one step, then another, then another. And when he reached the end, he looked up at me and whispered, "I can do all things through Christ who strengthens me."

That was it. Those simple words. But they carried the weight of his heart.

You're not weak for being overwhelmed; you're human for feeling the weight of what mattered."

In that moment, I realized that hope wasn't just in the progress—it was in the effort. It was in his determination. It was in the fight he still had inside him. And it was in the strength God was giving both of us to keep going.

Those moments of hope didn't erase the challenges, but they gave us something to hold onto. They reminded us that healing was happening, even if slowly. They reminded us that God was still present, still faithful, still working behind the scenes.

And they reminded me that pushing past the pain wasn't just my journey—it was ours.

"You haven't failed just because you're hurting. Pain is often the body's way of saying you've been strong for too long."

Looking back on that season, I realize now that pain didn't break me—it revealed me. It uncovered a strength I didn't know I had, a resilience I didn't know I carried, and a faith that was deeper than the storm I was facing. I didn't feel strong at the time. I didn't feel brave. I didn't feel prepared. But every day I kept moving, kept praying, kept believing, kept showing up. And that was enough.

Phillip's recovery taught me that healing is not a straight line. It's a journey of steps forward and steps back, of victories and setbacks, of tears and triumphs. But it also taught me that hope can survive even the hardest seasons. It can grow in hospital rooms. It can rise in rehab centers. It can live in whispered prayers and trembling hands. It can show up in the smallest moments and still change everything.

Balancing my new life, again ministry was my second job, being a mother, caregiving my husband and pastoring stretched me in ways I never imagined. It forced me to confront my limits, my fears, and my own humanity. But it also pushed me into a deeper dependence on God. I learned that His strength truly is made perfect in weakness—not in the absence of struggle, but right in the middle of it.

And Phillip… he showed me what courage looks like when life knocks you down. He showed me what determination looks like when your body won't cooperate. He showed me what faith looks like when you have to fight for every inch of progress. His journey reminded me that strength isn't always loud or visible. Sometimes it's quiet. Sometimes it's slow. Sometimes it's simply the decision to try again.

As a family, we didn't just survive that season—we grew through it. We learned to communicate differently. We learned to love out loud. We learned to lean on each other and on God in ways we never had before. And we learned that even when life changes without warning, God remains steady.

This chapter of my life—this chapter of *our* life—was painful, exhausting, and overwhelming. But it was also holy. It was a place where God met us, carried us, and shaped us. It was a place where I discovered the strength of a First Lady, the heart of a caregiver, the courage of a leader, and the endurance of a woman who refused to give up.

Pushing past the pain didn't mean ignoring it. It meant trusting that God could use it. And He did.

"Sometimes the purpose of pain is simply to push us toward a version of ourselves we wouldn't have met otherwise."

As I close this chapter, I carry with me the truth that pain may visit, but it does not have the final say. Purpose does. Faith does. Love does. And the God who brought me through that season is the same God who continues to lead me forward.

This is what it means to push past the pain: to rise, to endure, to believe, and to keep moving—one step, one prayer, one moment at a time.

Pastor's Wife there will be pain in your life and sometimes there is nothing you can do to prepare for it but just know that the Lord Jesus says in his word " He will never leave you nor forsake you" and he is El ROI – the God who sees you!

In my conclusion, "I push past the pain quietly, because I don't know how to explain the weight I'm carrying but I know who is carrying it with me" **"Thank You Jesus!"**

"Growth rarely announces itself—it often arrives disguised as discomfort."

About the Author

Dr. Jacqueline Renee Duncan is a dynamic woman of faith, purpose, and power. She is a wife, mother, pastor, prophetess, CEO, Author, Christian Chaplain, and Purpose Pusher who is passionate about helping others discover and fulfill their God-given purpose. Together with her husband, Apostle Phillip Duncan, she pastors In His Presence Praise and Worship Temple, a thriving apostolic ministry in Maryland.

Prophetess Jacqueline is the founder and CEO of Leading Ladies of Integrity Inc., an organization empowering pastors' wives and women in ministry. She is also a certified life coach, counselor, nutrition coach, and adult mental health aide, equipping individuals to live whole and healthy lives. Through her business, as the CEO of Purpose Pusher Inspire Coaching, LLC, she delivers bold, faith-based coaching that challenges others to walk fearlessly in their divine purpose.

A gifted communicator and accomplished author, Prophetess Jacqueline has written and co-authored several inspiring books, been featured on numerous media platforms, and is the host of The Jacqueline Renee Show Podcast. She serves as a founding member of the DMV Christian Chamber of Commerce. In 2024, in recognition of her outstanding leadership and community service, she was honored with the Presidential Lifetime Achievement Award.

A proud native of Clarksville, Tennessee, Prophetess Jacqueline Duncan is a devoted wife and the loving mother of one adult daughter, Shekinah.

Quitting? NOPE! That's NOT an Option!

Apostle Myra L. Davis-Bellinger

SECTION 1

The Pressure Nobody Talks About

As long as I can remember, I always knew two things about my life: I would preach the Gospel, and I would be a pastor's wife. I didn't run from it, resent it, or negotiate with God about it. I watched leaders closely, studied other pastors' wives, and embraced this calling with joy because I believed it was part of Heaven's blueprint for me.

But what I did not know was that this calling came with an alphabet nobody taught me.

The ABCs of a First Lady do not come with a class, a handbook, or a mentor assigned to walk you through each letter. There is no training manual for the silent expectations, the unspoken judgments, or the invisible warfare waiting on the other side of "Yes, Lord." No one prepared me for the emotional and spiritual weight of carrying and birthing alongside my husband—or how to support the vision while still tending to my own soul.

No one explained how to balance covering the church, loving the people, raising a family, fighting my own private battles, and still showing up with grace. No class warned me that no matter how much you sacrifice or how sincerely you love, some people will still believe you never get it right. No one explained how demonic setups disguise themselves as ministry demands—how small misunderstandings can become full-blown spiritual warfare designed to create distance between a husband and wife, even when intentions are pure.

There have been days I was judged, blamed, and spiritually misread for decisions I didn't make, motives I never had, and actions I never intended—simply because of the position I stood in. There were Sundays when I drove home ready to resign from everything and everybody except God. There were moments when I fought with everything in me to shield my children from becoming discouraged by the behavior of "church people" who should have been examples. And there were seasons when the weight of ministry sat on my chest like a stone, forcing me into an honest conversation with the Lord where I cried out, "Lord, I am not equipped for this!"

So yes—I have wanted to quit. Many times.

But one thing anchored me: my relationship with the Holy Spirit was solid long before I ever stepped into this role. He has been my Savior, yes, but also my Adonai—my Master, my Guide, my Help, my stability when emotions screamed, my clarity when confusion whispered, and my breath when ministry felt suffocating. He has always been everything I needed Him to be, exactly when I needed Him to be it.

Like Paul, once I hear from Him, I confer no more with flesh and blood. That reality has kept me standing.

Still, the pressure has been great. And if you, like me, have ever stood with your husband fighting a battle he never saw—or navigated consequences of decisions made in faith, frailty, or growth—or protected your family from storms they didn't create, or wondered why the warfare feels so targeted, let me tell you the truth: it is personal.

This is the pressure nobody talks about.

And if you've ever been tempted to give up under that pressure, lean in close—because these words are for you.

Quitting? Nope. Hell tried it, but it's not an option!

SECTION 2

The Real Enemy Behind the Pressure

Let me tell you something every mature, seasoned, anointed Leading Lady—or any leader—eventually learns: it's never really the people.

It may look like people.

It may sound like people.

It may even hurt like people.

But don't let your eyes deceive you.

Behind every discouragement, every unexpected attack, and every draining moment in ministry, there is always a deeper, darker agenda at work. The pressure you feel is not random—it is coordinated.

The Word of God makes it unmistakably clear:

"For our struggle is not against flesh and blood, but against the rulers, against the powers, against the world forces of this present darkness, against the spiritual forces of wickedness in the heavenly places."

— Ephesians 6:12 (AMP)

This is not emotional exaggeration.

This is spiritual reality.

The kingdom of darkness studies women like us—not because we are fragile, but because hell knows we are dangerous.

We birth vision.

We stand with vision.

We carry our husbands and families in prayer.

We guard the home.

We set atmospheres.

We shape generations.

Our voices are powerful.

Our presence is prophetic.

Our assignment is weighty.

This is why the enemy targets us so fiercely.

He hates marriages that reflect Christ.

He hates covenant leadership.

He hates intercession.

He hates unity in the home and in the church.

He hates influence—especially the influence of a woman who knows who she is, what she carries, and Who called her.

So, hear me clearly: many of the battles you face are not personal—they are strategic.

Yes, the enemy may use people.

Yes, he may use misunderstandings, immaturity, or insecurity.

Yes, he may even use emotional fatigue or pressure within your home.

But never forget this one truth:

The real target is not your feelings.

The real target is your assignment.

SECTION 3

Why Quitting Is Not an Option

One thing I know about God is this: where He guides, He provides. Whom He calls, He equips. If He assigned you to this season, this place, this mantle, then He has already given you the grace to carry it. You must square your shoulders and settle this truth in your spirit: while we carry the feminine expression of God's heart, we cannot afford to live ruled by emotion. You are graced for your assignment.

That is why quitting is not an option.

1. You are being attacked because you are essential.

Your assignment is generational. People watch how you love, endure, lead, pray, and rise after disappointment. Your obedience carries power. Your consistency teaches stability. Your endurance becomes legacy.

2. Your voice is a weapon.

Your words carry healing, wisdom, authority, and deliverance. When you speak, atmospheres shift. When you pray, chains break. When you advise, clarity comes. No wonder the enemy fights to silence you.

And let me be clear—when I say "Quitting? NOPE!" I am not being cute or catchy. This is not a slogan. It is a stance, a posture, a war cry from a woman who has survived too much to back up now.

NOPE means absolutely not.

NOPE means the devil does not get the final say.

NOPE means I refuse to bow to pressure, people, emotions, or seasons.

NOPE draws a bloodline around my purpose and announces that every assignment of hell stops here.

3. The pressure is proof of your value.

You do not attack what carries no treasure. Heaven trusts you. Hell fears you.

4. God does His best work in the press.

Remember Jesus in Gethsemane—the place of crushing. Even He felt the pressure to quit. The miracle happened because He didn't.

5. Quitting breaks more than a moment.

Quitting delays destiny and leaves your testimony unfinished. You are too valuable, too impactful, and too anointed to quit.

God has called you to finish.

SECTION 4

A Personal Letter of Strength

My Dear Sister,

Everything God has called you to do, He has also graced you to do. Grace is the supernatural ability of God empowering you to do what you cannot do alone. Feeling stretched or overwhelmed does not mean you are failing—it means God is preparing to show Himself strong in you.

You are not walking this assignment alone. There are sisters who understand the pressure, the tears, the warfare, and the victories that don't look like victories yet. There are Aarons and Hurs in the Spirit lifting your arms. There are intercessors praying prayers you no longer have strength to pray. Heaven has invested heavily in your assignment.

And hear this truth: the price is never greater than the reward, and you are stronger than you think. Don't give up. Don't quit.

You are right on the edge of something. Greatness is about to be revealed.

The Holy Spirit is present. He is with you when you speak with authority and with you when you sit quietly gathering yourself again. He is with you when you are confident and when you question everything.

You are seen.

You are upheld.

You are supported.

You are celebrated.

So take a breath and remind yourself:

I am graced for this.

I am equipped for this.

I am not alone in this.

I will finish.

Quitting? NOPE.

The God who called you will carry you—and complete what He started in you.

This may be your season of pressure, but pressure is the place where God produces power. As He strengthens you, don't keep that strength to yourself—pour it into another sister walking through her own unseen battles.

May these words anchor you, steady you, and remind you that **NOPE! Quitting is NOT an option!**

About the Author

Apostle Myra L. Davis-Bellinger is the Lead Pastor of City of God Ministries International, a published author, life coach, and the creator of the Breathe with Myra brand. With more than thirty years of experience in church leadership, ministry development, and spiritual formation, she has become a sought-after transformational speaker, preacher, and teacher across faith-based, nonprofit, and leadership sectors.

As the visionary behind Operation Raise the Standard and the Director of the LEAD Excellence Academy, Apostle Bellinger equips leaders with clarity, excellence, and Spirit-led strategy for effective ministry and leadership.

Her books—including the Breathe series and other inspirational works—are designed to ignite transformation, renew vision, and inspire believers to live with purpose, resilience, and spiritual alignment.

Through her preaching, teaching, and leadership initiatives, Apostle Bellinger continues to empower individuals and leaders to pursue God's purpose with faith, wisdom, and excellence.

Resilience – Still Standing

By Lady Rhoda Kudawoo

Introduction – The Palm Tree

There is an old African adage that says, "The palm tree bends in the storm, but it does not break. It returns taller, its roots deeper." This is a wise saying with a deeper meaning. In many parts of Africa, the palm tree is more than just a plant—it is a symbol. It stands tall and graceful, its fronds dancing even in the fiercest winds. But what makes the palm tree truly remarkable is not its height or beauty; it is the way it survives storms.

When violent winds rage and the rains pour down, the palm tree does not resist. It bends, it yields, it lowers itself to the pressure, but it does not break. And when the storm has passed, it rises again—taller, more flexible, and often stronger than before.

The role of a First Lady is often admired from a distance. In ministry, we are often expected to stand tall, graceful, and composed just like the palm. We host, we serve, we intercede, we support, we lead, and we love—and yet behind the elegance is the strength needed to withstand, because this calling comes with storms: criticism, weariness, misunderstanding, grief, spiritual warfare, and unseen sacrifices.

Resilience, by definition, is the ability to recover quickly from difficulties. For the First Lady, it is more than recovery; it is the holy resolve to continue leading when you are tired, to keep loving when you are wounded, to keep standing when everything inside you wants to sit down. Resilience is not just bouncing back; it is growing deeper. It is bending without breaking. It is becoming wiser, stronger, and more anointed—not despite the storm, but because of it.

I have lived the bending seasons—the ones that humble you, stretch you, and make you feel invisible or misunderstood. I have learned how to bend without breaking, how to bow in prayer, and how to surrender in pain. But I have also experienced the miracle of rising again—not because I am immune to pain, but because I am rooted in God, who designed me to survive storms. Resilience is not just something I developed; it is something I have had to embody.

This chapter goes beyond my experiences; it is about every woman who bends under the weight of expectation but keeps showing up. It is a reminder that storms will come—but you, dear sister, are designed to survive them. You are rooted in something greater than the wind. You are made to bend, graced to rise. You are resilient.

The Role and the Rain – Why the Storms Come

To admire a palm tree from a distance is to see its grace. To stand under one during a storm is to see its strength. The same can be said for the role of a First Lady, or any woman in a position that requires resilience. To many, it looks like a crown—an honorable position beside the pastor, always poised, polished, and prayerful. But behind the scenes, it often feels more like a cross that must be carried.

The reality is this: the role invites the rain—not just a light drizzle, but most often torrential downpours. There is criticism that comes without cause, expectations that feel impossible to meet, the loneliness of leadership, and the pressure to be everything for everyone, all while silently fighting battles of your own. There are moments when ministry feels more like survival than service.

But just as the palm tree is native to climates known for their storms, the First Lady is often planted in environments where pressure is part of the call. This is not by accident; it is by design. God did not choose us for this role because we were unshakable, but because He knew we would hold on even when shaken.

The storm does not disqualify you. In fact, it often confirms your assignment. The rain does not ruin the palm tree; on the contrary, it helps it grow. So it is with you.

When your life is built on the Rock, the rain may fall, but you will not. You may bend, but you will not break. Resilience is not the absence of storms; it is the ability to stand in them. As a First Lady, you are not just standing—you are serving, leading, building, and loving through them.

You may bend under the weight of ministry, but you are rooted. And because you are rooted, you will not break. As Matthew 7:25 says, "The rain came down, the streams rose, and the winds blew and beat against that house; yet it did not fall, because it had its foundation on the rock."

The Bending – When It Looks Like It Might Break

The most misunderstood part of the palm tree's strength is in its flexibility. To an untrained eye, bending looks like weakness, surrender, or collapse. But in truth, the ability to bend is the very thing that keeps the tree alive during violent winds. It yields so it won't snap; it bows so it can stand again. That is not fragility—that's resilience by divine design.

There are seasons in your journey when you will not feel strong. You will bend under the weight of spiritual pressure, emotional exhaustion, and personal battles no one can see. But remember that you are not breaking—you are bending. And in the bending, you are being built, shaped, refined, and rooted deeper. Resilience is not about never feeling like you are going to fall apart. It is about choosing not to stay down when life knocks the wind out of you. It is about learning to bow in prayer, bend in surrender, and rise in power.

As Paul writes in 2 Corinthians 4:8–9, "We are hard pressed on every side, but not crushed; perplexed, but not in despair; persecuted but not abandoned; struck down but not destroyed."

This is the spiritual elasticity God gives us not to avoid storms, but to withstand them. Bending teaches us to be humble, to depend on God, to recognize that our strength is not in how loudly we lead but in how deeply we trust in Him. So if you find yourself in a season of bending, take heart. You are not weak, you are not failing, you are not breaking, you are being made resilient.

The Roots – What Keeps You Grounded

The secret of the palm tree's survival is not in its height, but in its roots. While the world marvels at how tall it stands, what sustains it is what lies beneath the surface. Palm trees have root systems that stretch wide and deep, anchoring them securely even in loose, sandy soil. They do not look for fame underground; they look for stability.

That is the hidden strength of a First Lady: deep roots. Ministry will expose where your roots truly lie. Title alone will not hold you. Public honor will not anchor you. Shallow applause fades quickly when the storms of real life and spiritual warfare roll in. What sustains you, what truly makes you resilient, is not how visible you are, but how rooted you are.

For me, my roots have grown deeper through pain, pressure, and perseverance. My personal relationship with God has been my lifeline—the Word of God, prayer, and fasting. Before I ever stand beside a pulpit, I kneel in prayer. When I feel unseen by people, I draw strength from being fully seen by Him. My secret place has become my safe place.

In addition to God, my roots include wise counsel and trusted voices who do not just cheer me on publicly but cover me privately—people who know when to pray, when to listen, and when to say, "Rest." These roots may not be seen, but they are necessary for your survival. Because when the storm comes—and it always will—what keeps me from breaking is not what people see; it is what God sees. The deeper the root, the higher the rise. If you want to endure in this calling, you must stay rooted in Christ, in truth, in purpose, and in love.

The Rise – Standing Again, Even Taller

After the storm, the bent tree returns strengthened. The winds that looked like they might destroy it only helped deepen its roots and stretch its structure. That is what resilience does. It does not just help you survive; it helps you grow. As First Ladies, we do not just rise because the storm ends; we rise because God lifts us. We rise because grace is not just given to us to endure—we are empowered to overcome.

Every time we rise again after loss, after burnout, after criticism, or after heartbreak, we carry something new: wisdom, compassion, and fresh oil.

Resilience is a refining fire. It burns away pride, reveals purpose, teaches patience, and brings clarity. It shows you where your strength really lies—not in people, not in position, but in the presence of God. When a First Lady rises, it is not just for herself. Your rising becomes a testimony for those who watched you bend. Your rising becomes hope for other women in ministry. Your rising becomes evidence that God is still faithful even in storms. So yes, you may have bent. But look at you now—still rooted, still fruitful, still rising.

A Word to the Weary – You Will Not Break

Dear Woman of God, if you are reading this and feel like you are at the breaking point—if the weight of ministry, life, marriage, or motherhood is pressing so hard you can barely breathe—I want you to pause and remember this: You are the palm tree. You may bend, but you will not break.

You are not alone. So many of us have stood where you are—holding back tears while holding up others, pouring into others while feeling empty yourself. But the very fact that you are still here, still showing up, still loving, still leading, is proof of your resilience.

You may feel bent under the pressure right now. But what you may not see is how your roots are growing deeper, how your strength is being fortified, and how your faith is being refined. And just like the palm tree, you will rise again—not just restored, but renewed. This is not your breaking; this is your becoming.

Rest when you need to. Cry when you must. But never forget—you were built for this. You are graced for this. You are resilient.

This page intentionally left blank

About the Author

Lady Rhoda Kudawoo is a woman of integrity and vision who serves as First Lady and Co-Pastor of House of Joy Global Ministries. She is a passionate advocate for marriage and is committed to guiding couples toward Christ-centered relationships.

As an author and sought-after conference speaker, Lady Rhoda empowers women to embrace their God-given potential and walk confidently in their purpose. She is also the founder of The Rhoyal Collection, a brand that beautifully blends modest fashion with faith.

A devoted wife, mother of six, and ministry leader, Lady Rhoda exemplifies grace, resilience, and purpose. Through her life and ministry, she inspires others to live boldly for Christ and to make a lasting impact for the Kingdom of God.

Service – Not Called to Serve Here, There, and Everywhere

By Pastor Sandra P. Lilly

Introduction: The Misconception of Omnipresence

The first-century Apostles did not serve here, there, and everywhere. We read about them. We celebrate and revere who they were and how they were used by God. But what is generally glossed over is that they had divine purpose and specificity on their lives. They each were born with God-given gifts, talents, and abilities that differed from one another. They were born and raised in different areas and families, and yet, through the totality of who they were, God's highest purposes for their lives were realized.

Their understanding of what their purposes were did not become clear to them until Christ came into their lives. And that began the specificity of their purposes, assignments, and fulfillment. During the early church age, little was recorded about church leadership, practical functioning, and assignments. There were a few mandates set down for leadership and their wives, but nothing about the purposes of God being in both of them (the two becoming one flesh) and being worked out and manifested through God using both of them.

Perhaps due to the cultural norms of those times, there was no joint preparation of husbands and wives for ministry. It appears there was no seeking for what was inside of that marriage that God was calling forth for His purpose and for His Kingdom-building purposes. Perhaps this is the root from which contemporary church operation grew, along with the expectation that pastors' wives should be everywhere doing many things.

In some settings, she serves merely as a physical presence beside her husband. In others, she is a full-time homemaker, mother, church administrator, counselor, spiritual leader, and often an unpaid laborer for countless ministries.

The Weight of Expectation

The pressure to serve "everywhere" comes from every direction: the husband, church leadership, denominational authorities, the congregation, the community, and even family members. As a pastor's wife, overhearing conversations about what "your role" should be can stir a whirlwind of emotions—hurt, isolation, anger, being misunderstood, or a desire to withdraw.

But who set these expectations? Where did they come from? And more importantly—are they even biblical?

There is no commandment in Scripture that states, "Thou shalt serve in all roles, at all times, to please all people." Yet many of us have been used, used up, abused, hurt, and disrespected in ways we seldom admit out loud. We carry those wounds into our homes, our prayer closets, and our callings. Sometimes, we just want to run, hide, leave, and never come back.

Returning to the Word

Psalm 56:9 reminds us, "This I know: God is for me." We are not forgotten or forsaken. We are fearfully and wonderfully made—crafted by God with intentionality. Our lives, including our roles in ministry, are not accidents. We are not placeholders, stand-ins, or church props. We were created for purpose.

Jeremiah 1:5 declares, "Before I formed you in the womb, I knew you." This is more than poetic—it is a statement of divine intent. God infused us with gifts, talents, abilities, intelligences, dispositions, personalities, and even callings. We were born with Kingdom purpose—not just to support, but to lead, create, build, and transform.

This message isn't just theological—it's personal. I know, because I've lived it.

I have been a pastor's wife for over forty years. I received Jesus as Savior at age nine and was raised in and served in church all of my young life. While young, I made a decision to only marry a Christian man. We were both Christians from the start, but there was never a life in pastoral ministry in view.

Six years into our marriage, my husband was called to preach, and that changed the whole trajectory of both of our lives. No one in either of our families was in ministry. This was an unexpected shift away from our intense business and career pursuits to a walk into my husband's calling into Christian ministry.

I began to intensely look for and voraciously read books to find examples to follow. I tried to emulate things that I saw and some of what I read. Some of it suited me, and some of it didn't. I immaturely thought my sincere efforts to work and labor for the church and its people would be well received, but that wasn't the case.

I received pressure to serve excessively in multiple roles and still take care of my husband, home, children, and professional teaching job. All of the wise counsel available at that time was from ministry traditionalists who believed the husband was called and the wife was not. Wives were limited and boxed into being chaste keepers at home, mothers, and serving workers at the church.

There was no notion that God was fulfilling His purpose to use the two who became one to fulfill His whole purpose—using both of them to grow and develop whole people and whole churches through which He could save, heal, and develop Christians who would fulfill their own God-given purposes in life as an honor unto the Lord Jesus Christ.

How much hurt, pain, conflict, separation, and even divorce and craziness would have been avoided if God's purposed intent over the two becoming one had been understood? Many of us have experienced a model in which the pastor's gifts were preferred over the truth that God's purposes were placed on both of them when He brought them together in marriage and ministry.

The cacophony of voices and requests—sometimes even whispered— places more expectations on pastors' wives. Is there a place in the New Testament, in the beginning of the church age, where our traditional paradigm is mandated and pastors were separate from their wives in divine purpose?

Aquila and Priscilla: A Model of Ministry Agreement

Thankfully, the Bible gives us a powerful example of what divine purpose looks like when two become one in agreement. Aquila and Priscilla are more than a footnote in the early church—they are a divine model of shared ministry.

They were a married couple, united not only in love, but in purpose. Scripture tells us they were tentmakers by trade (Acts 18:3), but their work together extended far beyond the marketplace. Through their personal relationships with God, they each came into clarity about their gifts and callings. What is remarkable is that they didn't operate separately. They chose agreement.

Together, Aquila and Priscilla discerned that all of who they were— individually and collectively—was part of God's original purpose for their lives. Their skills, insights, and spiritual gifts didn't cancel each other out; they completed each other. They understood that God was not just using Aquila as "the head" and Priscilla as "the help." He was using all of both of them to fulfill one Kingdom purpose.

It was through that holy agreement and alignment that their ministry flourished. They didn't just support the Apostle Paul—they housed him, ministered beside him, and were entrusted with deep theological truths. In fact, Priscilla—named first in Romans 16:3 and Acts 18:26—helped teach and correct Apollos, a powerful male preacher, alongside her husband. This wasn't by accident. It was by divine design.

In 1 Corinthians 16:19, 2 Timothy 4:19, and Acts 18, they are consistently presented as a couple who worked together in ministry and demonstrated their faith in Christ through teaching, traveling with Apostle Paul, showing hospitality, acts of service, and even hosting a church in their house.

Their lifelong united service in ministry shows the integration of purpose between husband and wife—joining their gifts, strengths, and talents together to accomplish God's assignment upon both of their lives and ministry. They served together by love, purpose, and agreement.

When we look closely, Aquila and Priscilla represent a divine partnership—two people whose unity, agreement, and spiritual purpose made room for multiplied impact. God used them to teach, build, lead, and guide others into the fullness of Christ—not because one had the spotlight while the other stood silently behind, but because they moved in harmony, letting the Spirit of God use every part of who they were as one.

Their story invites us to ask: What if God's true design for pastoral couples was never division of labor, but divine unity of purpose?

Conclusion: Purpose Over Performance

We must remember—God never called us to exhaustion; He called us to excellence. His glory is revealed not through our ability to be everywhere at once, but through our faithfulness in the assignments He has specifically entrusted to us. A pastor's wife is not simply an accessory to ministry; she is a vessel chosen, equipped, and anointed for Kingdom impact in her own right.

When we walk in agreement with our spouses and in alignment with God's purposes, we become unstoppable forces for His glory. So let us reject the myth of serving here, there, and everywhere, and instead embrace the joy of serving exactly where He has called us—fully present, fully purposed, and fully His.

This page intentionally left blank

About the Author

Pastor Sandra P. Lilly is a teacher, ministry leader, author, and conference founder with more than four decades of service in church leadership. Alongside her husband, Pastor James E. Lilly Jr., she has faithfully served as a pastor's wife and ministry partner for over 40 years. In 1992, they co-founded Eagles Summit Christian Fellowship Church in Durham, North Carolina, where she serves as Co-Founder and Chief Operating Officer.

Pastor Lilly holds a Bachelor of Science in Education from Temple University in Philadelphia and completed post-graduate studies at Marywood College in Pennsylvania. She served for 22 years as a public-school teacher, developing a passion for education, mentoring, and leadership development that continues to shape her ministry.

She is the co-author of The Master's Class, a leadership development course designed for both ministry and corporate environments. She is also the founder of the Women of Success Conference and the R.E.F.R.E.S.H. Women's Ministry, which equips women to become "Restored Enough For Relationships that are Encouraging, Supportive, and Healthy."

A gifted teacher, trainer, worship leader, and lifelong singer, Pastor Lilly is passionate about leadership development, marriage and family restoration, and helping women recover from abuse and trauma. She is the mother of two daughters and the proud grandmother of two.

Tenacity Unleashed

by Lady Phyllis Gerald

Tenacity – the unyielding, persistent determination to achieve goals and overcome adversity; an *unstoppable force* of human resilience.

"I press toward the mark for the prize of the high calling of God in Christ Jesus." — Philippians 3:14

Introduction: The Authority of Five Years

I do not write this chapter as a seasoned matriarch of ministry or as one who has decades of pastoral scars and triumphs to draw from. I write as a woman who has been a pastor's wife for five years—long enough to be tested, stretched, misunderstood, refined, and still standing, but short enough to remember clearly the momentum shift of the calling.

My authority is not longevity; it is lived obedience, a driving force led by the Spirit of God and accompanied by many tears and sleepless nights of praying.

At the same time, my five years have not been lived in isolation. For more than twenty years, I have walked alongside and served pastors' wives—listening, learning, interceding, and observing patterns of grace, endurance, burnout, restoration, and yes, even their heartache and tears.

Long before I carried this title personally, I carried these women in prayer and proximity. That vantage point has given me reverence for the weight of this calling and compassion for those who bear it.

Tenacity, from this combined perspective, is not about mastering ministry culture or perfecting resilience. It is about staying when expectations are unclear, when identity feels compressed, and when obedience costs more than anticipated.

Five years in, I have learned that tenacity is not loud. It is quiet, daily, Spirit-dependent endurance.

This chapter is for the pastor's wife who is still becoming—who is still learning the terrain of ministry while guarding her soul.

Tenacity in Identity

In the world's language, tenacity is aggressive perseverance. In ministry, tenacity is holy restraint paired with unwavering commitment. It is faithfulness to God, to marriage, and to personal stewardship when pressure threatens all three.

Tenacity is not saying yes to everything. It is discerning what belongs to you and what belongs to God.

I believe many pastors' wives burn out not from lack of passion but from misunderstanding perseverance. Tenacity is not proving your worth; it is refusing to abandon your assignment.

One of my first tests of tenacity was identity disruption.

Overnight, you are no longer simply yourself—you are now "the pastor's wife." Expectations, spoken and unspoken, attempt to define you.

Tenacity in this season has meant resisting two different temptations:

- Silencing my voice to avoid pressure
- Performing to meet it

Being anchored in my identity in Christ rather than congregational approval is a mantra I once struggled with but now live by.

If identity is not guarded early, ministry will define you in ways God never intended.

I have personally witnessed many pastors' wives operating under that pressure.

Tenacity says: **"I will not lose myself to fulfill a role."**

Tenacity in Marriage Under Ministry Pressure

Marriage often becomes the silent battleground of ministry.

Schedules, planning, emotional demands, and spiritual warfare all collide from every side—often without warning.

If we are not careful, the pressure can deplete us and even lead to discouragement or depression.

At times I felt unseen—not from a lack of love, although it can feel that way—but because of the weight ministry placed on my husband and on my own emotional capacity.

Daily posture had to become intentional.

Tenacity requires honest and open communication—almost like learning a new language.

Staying committed to "us" while honoring "the call" is another dimension of endurance and God's grace.

Let's Talk About Tenacity in Loneliness

Loneliness is one of the least acknowledged realities for pastors' wives.

You can be surrounded by people yet still lack a true outlet.

Thankfully, God allowed me to be that safe space for other pastors' wives before becoming one myself. That place of confidentiality taught me early how important trusted relationships are.

At the same time, confidentiality can restrict vulnerability, and the calling can reshape friendships.

Loneliness tested my tenacity more than people's opinions.

Whether introverted or extroverted, I have learned to be alone without becoming isolated and be settled without becoming invisible.

Tenacity requires cultivating a private life with God strong enough to sustain a public life in ministry.

Seeking safe relationships outside the immediate church context can sometimes feel uncomfortable, but it is often necessary.

Personally, I am thankful for the friendships where I can say:

"I need to talk… I need to cry… I need sharpening."

These are relationships that do not treat me differently when the door opens for me to walk publicly.

Criticism Without Hardening

Criticism—wow, let's talk about it.

Some criticism is fair. Some is unfounded. Some is painful.

Why? Because it often comes from people you served sincerely.

Tenacity does not mean developing thick skin at the expense of a soft heart.

If we are not careful, our hearts will harden and bitterness will take root.

I have learned to discern what to receive and what to release, to allow God to defend what He assigned, and to resist unnecessary self-justification.

Criticism can refine us, but it should never define our identity.

Never forget:

Only God justifies and identifies.

Spiritual Warfare and Tenacity Power

Spiritual warfare is real—very real—and often subtle.

It can manifest through:

- fatigue
- discouragement

- oppression
- misunderstandings
- comparison
- being disgruntled
- lack of self-care

Your spiritual life can quietly erode if you are not careful.

Tenacity means showing up consistently.

Praying when you don't feel God.

Worshiping when your heart feels heavy.

Standing when nothing seems to be manifesting in the natural.

Faithfulness develops spiritual rhythms—the press that eventually leads to the fulfillment of the promise:

A table prepared before you in the presence of your enemies.

The Grace of Remaining in the Process

Five years have taught me humility.

I do not know everything.

I have not seen every season.

Tenacity does not require pretending to be seasoned—it requires teachability and obedience.

God is not impressed by overextension.

He honors faithfulness.

I have learned that saying, *"I am still learning,"* is wisdom, not weakness.

Whether through intercession, discernment, or quiet obedience, tenacity is often exercised behind the scenes before it is ever seen.

I have also learned the importance of boundaries.

Self-care is stewardship—not selfishness.

Tenacity required learning to say no without guilt, scheduling rest intentionally, and guarding emotional and spiritual margins.

Longevity is built through sustainability and thriving, not just survival.

A Personal Testimony of Tenacity

There have been many moments during these five years when I realized tenacity would not look like triumph—it would look like choice.

The choice to stay present when I felt unsure.

The choice to remain prayerful when answers were slow.

The choice to stay soft and gracious when retreat felt safer.

I have not remained because I am strong.

I remained because God is faithful.

Again and again, He has met me in the trenches and in the ordinary faithfulness of simply showing up.

He continues to reshape my expectations, steady my heart, and teach me that obedience does not require clarity—only trust.

Conclusion: The Staying Power of Tenacity

Five years have not completed my story.

They have only anchored my resolve.

I am still here—not because it has been easy, but because God has been faithful.

Choosing obedience over approval and trust over control—that is tenacity.

When you are unleashed into your divine purpose by the hand of God, a power emerges that is unstoppable.

You do not need decades to be legitimate.

You need devotion, discernment, and the courage to stay present in the process.

Tenacity is not about how long you have served.

It is about resilience—the grit to keep moving forward when it feels like you are riding a tricycle up Mount Everest.

It is about how faithfully you walk with God while you are becoming.

No Present Without a Past

I carry deep respect for the pastors' wives and godly women who mentored me.

Their wisdom shaped me long before I stepped into this role officially.

But God made it clear that I could not live off borrowed oil forever.

Knowing about ministry and carrying ministry are two very different things.

When the weight settled on my shoulders, I realized that experience does not exempt you from stretching seasons.

Tenacity became the grace to be confident in what God had taught me while remaining humble enough to admit I was still learning.

Tenacity meant honoring what had been poured into me while embracing my own voice, boundaries, and rhythms.

Imitation can inspire—but authenticity sustains.

God was not asking me to replicate anyone else's ministry.

He was asking me to steward mine faithfully.

Standing in my own calling required courage.

Unleashing tenacity gave me permission to grow into this role at God's pace.

Stand sure.

DECLARE TODAY

TENACITY IS UNLEASHED IN ME!

About the Author

Lady Phyllis Gerald serves at The Meeting Place Worship Center in Huntsville, Alabama, alongside her husband, Bishop Anthony Gerald. She is a devoted servant-leader, Biblical Life Coach, and CEO of Her Divine Connection, with a deep passion and divine calling to win souls and empower women to walk boldly in their God-given purpose.

Her ministry is rooted in Kingdom living and focuses on equipping women who are called to ministry to operate in spiritual demonstration and power without fear or limitation.

Through prayer, biblical teaching, and prophetic encouragement, Lady Phyllis inspires others to grow in faith, lead with confidence, and build strong families and thriving church communities.

Understanding Is Power!

By Apostle Cynthia Brazelton

One of my favorite stories in the Bible is the Parable of the Sower. This parable is found in three Gospels—Matthew, Mark, and Luke—and it is one of the most powerful illustrations Jesus ever gave. It has changed my life, and I believe it can change yours as well.

In Mark 4:13, Jesus makes a striking statement about this parable: "If you don't understand this parable, how will you understand any of the parables?" In other words, the Parable of the Sower is foundational. If we cannot grasp this, we will struggle to understand how the Kingdom of God operates.

At its core, Jesus explains that "the sower sows the Word" (Mark 4:14). This reveals a powerful principle: the Kingdom of God does not function by human effort, striving, or religious activity. In this Kingdom, it isn't merely what we do that produces results, but how we receive, believe, and engage with the Word of God—with understanding.

Matthew's Gospel brings even greater clarity. Jesus says:

"For the hearts of this people have grown dull. Their ears are hard of hearing, and their eyes they have closed, lest they should see with their eyes and hear

with their ears, lest they should understand with their hearts and turn, so that I should heal them" (Matthew 13:15 NKJV).

Then, explaining the parable, He continues:

"When anyone hears the word of the kingdom and does not understand it, then the wicked one comes and snatches away what was sown in his heart" (Matthew 13:18–19 NKJV).

Notice this: the Word of God has limitless potential, but without understanding, the enemy can snatch it away before it takes root. The battlefield is not just in what we hear, but in what we comprehend and embrace with our hearts.

That is why understanding is so vital. Seeing, hearing, and understanding the Word becomes the pathway to success in every area of our lives. It is in the heart where you and I come to truly grasp the limitless possibilities of God's Word. And once that Word is understood, nothing can stop it from producing results.

Understanding: The Bridge to Results

Understanding is power. It is the unseen force that undergirds our actions and determines our results. We prosper, not by chance, but on the strength of our understanding. Nothing in ministry, in business, in relationships, or in life happens without it.

Think about it: our actions are only outlets—expressions of what we understand. If there is no true understanding behind what we do, our efforts become empty motions, lacking fruit. That is why I believe the bridge between desire and the fulfillment of that desire is called understanding. Desire alone cannot produce results; it must be connected to understanding.

But what exactly is understanding? It is not just intellectual knowledge. It is spiritual and practical—a divine comprehension that shapes how we live, how we decide, and how we walk with God and with others. Understanding is the working application of God's Word in our lives. It is the light that turns knowledge into direction and wisdom into action.

The Bible emphasizes this truth:

- *"Wisdom is the principal thing; therefore get wisdom. And in all your getting, get understanding"* (Proverbs 4:7 NKJV). Wisdom without understanding cannot bear fruit.

- *"Through wisdom a house is built, and by understanding it is established"* (Proverbs 24:3 NKJV). Wisdom lays the foundation, but understanding secures it.

- *"Good understanding gains favor"* (Proverbs 13:15 NKJV). Favor flows not just from effort, but from understanding.

Notice that wisdom and knowledge are often celebrated, but Scripture insists on something deeper: understanding. Knowledge is information, wisdom is insight, but understanding is application—it is the ability to connect truth to life in a way that produces results.

Understanding Is Spiritually Unlocked

Understanding is not something we gain through study alone. It is given by God.

Luke 24:45 (TPT) says, "He supernaturally unlocked their understanding to receive the revelation of the Scriptures." After Jesus' resurrection, the disciples had knowledge of His teachings and memories of His words, but until He unlocked their understanding, they could not see the full picture of God's plan.

This shows us a vital truth: understanding is a spiritual gift. It is the Spirit of God who illuminates our minds, makes Scripture alive, and helps us rightly discern situations. Without God opening our understanding, the Bible can remain a closed book, life can feel confusing, and our decisions may lack clarity. But when God unlocks our understanding, His Word becomes revelation, and our steps become ordered.

Paul prayed for this very thing. In Ephesians 1:17–18 (NIV), he asked that God would give believers "the Spirit of wisdom and revelation, so that you may know Him better. I pray that the eyes of your heart may be enlightened in order that you may know the hope to which He has called you." Notice again—understanding is not simply mental, but spiritual. It is the enlightening of the heart.

The Example of Solomon

King Solomon is remembered as the wisest king who ever lived, not because he asked for riches, power, or long life, but because he asked God for an understanding heart.

In 1 Kings 3:9 (NLT), Solomon prayed:

"Give me an understanding heart so that I can govern your people well and know the difference between right and wrong."

God was so pleased with Solomon's request that He not only gave him wisdom and understanding but also added wealth and honor (1 Kings 3:11–14). Solomon's reign flourished because he valued understanding above personal gain.

What can we learn here? When we pursue understanding—when we seek God's perspective instead of just human success—we position ourselves for blessings beyond measure.

Jesus and the Disciples

Even Jesus' disciples struggled with understanding. In Mark 8:16–21, when they worried about not having bread, Jesus rebuked them: "Don't you know or understand even yet? Are your hearts too hard to take it in? You have eyes—can't you see? You have ears—can't you hear?"

They had witnessed miracles, seen bread multiplied before their very eyes, and yet they still missed the lesson. The issue was not the absence of miracles—it was the absence of understanding.

This is the same danger we face today. We may attend church, hear sermons, and witness God's provision, yet still fail to grasp the spiritual meaning behind His works. Without understanding, we miss what God is doing right in front of us.

Understanding in Real Life

1. In Marriage

Many couples love each other, but love without understanding often leads to frustration and separation. Love may draw two people together, but it is understanding that sustains the relationship.

1 Peter 3:7 tells husbands to "dwell with them with understanding." Without understanding, a spouse may feel unheard or unappreciated. But when couples choose to view situations through the Word and seek relational understanding from Scripture, love grows stronger.

2. In Business

Many businesses fail not because of a lack of passion but because of a lack of understanding—of finances, timing, and people. Passion without understanding can lead to poor decisions. But when we pray for understanding, God provides insight into strategy, stewardship, and timing.

3. In Ministry

Ministry requires passion, but passion without understanding leads to burnout and misdirection. Understanding reveals the importance of delegation, boundaries, and focusing on God's priorities.

4. In Trials

Trials often bring confusion, but Proverbs 3:5–6 instructs us to trust in the Lord rather than lean on our own understanding. Divine understanding allows us to see beyond present pain into God's eternal purpose.

What Understanding Produces

1. Clarity in Decision-Making
2. Stability in Life
3. Fruitfulness in Ministry
4. Favor with God and Man

How to Grow in Understanding

1. Ask God for It (James 1:5)
2. Meditate on God's Word (Psalm 119:130)
3. Depend on the Holy Spirit (John 16:13)
4. Walk with Wise People (Proverbs 13:20)

Closing Prayer

Pray daily: "Lord, give me an understanding heart. Help me to see what I do not see, to know what I do not know, and to grasp Your will with clarity. Let my actions be fueled by true understanding, so that my life may produce the results You have destined for me. In Jesus' name!"

When you walk in understanding, you will not stumble in confusion. You will prosper in your calling, bear fruit in your labor, and experience the fulfillment of God's promises in every area of your life.

This page intentionally left blank

About the Author

Apostle Cynthia Brazelton and her husband, Tony, serve as Pastors and Apostles of Victory Christian Ministries International (VCMI), a family-oriented church focused on nurturing spirit, soul, and body. They have four children: Tony Jr., Antoinette, Jordan, and Aaron. VCMI is a non-denominational, multi-racial church with multiple locations across Maryland, Washington D.C., Virginia, Florida, and the United Kingdom.

The Brazeltons are also dedicated to helping other pastors through Tony and Cynthia Brazelton Ministries Sons and Daughters (TCBMSD), which connects over 50 ministries for spiritual guidance. Apostle Cynthia emphasizes the importance of manifesting God's power in everyday life, urging believers to engage deeply with the Word of God.

She believes that understanding God's Word leads to personal transformation, enabling individuals to strengthen others in faith, as articulated in 1 John 4:17: "As He (Jesus) is, so are we in this world." Apostle Cynthia holds a unique anointing to teach and support women, evident in her founding of Virtuous Women's Conference International (VWCI), where she inspires thousands globally through various conferences and events.

VCMI.ORG | TCBM.ORG

Voices of Wisdom & Truth

By Dr. Barbara Layton

As parents, one of our greatest responsibilities is the nurturing and care of our children. Being entrusted with their physical health, emotional health, as well as spiritual health requires time and patience—time that on some days you feel like you don't have, and other days when your patience gets stretched to its limit. As a mother of seven children, I've experienced many days like these when I needed just a little more time to complete my day, and other days when I needed just a little more time and patience to satisfy everyone's needs for my attention.

Some days were smoother than others, but the intense days could really be intense—especially when each child has a different temperament, which requires a slightly different approach to communication and discipline. The melancholy child refuses to share their true feelings and thoughts. The choleric child needs social interaction and intellectual engagement. The sanguine child is also very social with a need to be the center of attention. And let's not forget the supine and the phlegmatic. What a blessing from God children are, designed in His image and entrusted to our care as parents.

In the book of Psalms 127:3 (NKJV) it says:

"Behold, children are a heritage from the Lord, the fruit of the womb is a reward. Like arrows in the hand of a warrior, so are the children of one's youth."

Our children are a blessing—a gift of love from God to us—and we as parents must use our voices, along with the Voice of Truth from God's Word, to direct their paths.

When our children are young, we are the voice of comfort, ensuring them that they are protected and safe. We are the voice of guidance, always there to provide direction and counsel. We are the advocate, supporting them and being their number one cheerleader, but also correcting them when correction is required. We are the voice of reason when they are in disputes with their siblings, helping them make peaceful resolutions. Constantly imparting wisdom and direction, we fulfill their needs with love and compassion.

Each time we speak, they recognize our voices. Love is conveyed through our voices. Peace is received through our voices, and directions are followed. They recognize and understand our love for them through our voices. Helping our children navigate through life is a job entrusted to all parents by God.

Proverbs 22:6 (Passion Translation) says:

"Dedicate your children to God and point them in the way that they should go, and the values they've learned from you will be with them for life."

In prayer we receive understanding of our assignment—to dedicate and commit our children to the Lord, preparing them to hear the Voice of Truth and making them aware of His presence in their everyday lives.

Today we are invaded with voices that speak into the lives of our children at an accelerated speed compared to five to ten years ago. These voices come in the form of social media outlets such as Facebook, Twitter, Messenger, and YouTube. These outlets are all competing for prominence in the lives of our children, all desiring the right to be heard—or should I say to be "liked" and "shared."

Being unaware of these potentially harmful platform voices can and will override our voices of influence as parents if left unchecked and ignored. Understanding social media voices is something we as parents must be aware of before they establish prominence in the lives of our children.

Here are a few ways that social media outlets could potentially affect our children's ability to hear our voices:

- By isolating them for hours and hours a day from their source of stability.

- By exposing them to cyberbullying—children are easily hurt when faced with experiences that attack their self-esteem. Without our voices of love and reassurance, fear and self-doubt can attach themselves to them.

- By exposing them to ungodly content such as violence, sexual material, and illegal activity. This exposure can cause anxiety and depression, thus establishing strongholds of influence designed to block our voices.

Jesus said, *"My sheep hear my voice, and a stranger they will not follow."*

John 10:5 (Amplified Bible) says:

"They will never (on any account) follow a stranger, but will run away from him because they do not know the voice of strangers or recognize their call."

It is our responsibility to introduce our children to God and to share His love for them. As we equip our children with the confidence and assurance that God loves them through the voice of His Word, unconditional love is understood and received, and trust is established.

John 3:16 (New King James Version) says:

"For God so loved the world that He gave His only begotten Son, that whosoever believes in Him should not perish, but have everlasting life."

1 John 4:9 (Amplified Bible) says:

"In this the love of God was made manifest (displayed) where we are concerned, in that God sent His Son, the only begotten or unique Son, into the world so that we might live through Him."

Just as God loved us, we must always remember that same love must be established in the training of our children.

Jesus promised never to leave us, but to send another Helper. The Holy Spirit—the Voice of Truth—will speak to our children about how special they are in His sight. I want to convey how important our voices as parents are in shaping the ability of children to hear the voice of the Holy Spirit. We must be intentional in sharing the Word of God—whether through daily devotionals, children's Bible stories, games, or music—to bring understanding of the love of God.

John 14:15–16 (The Passion Translation) says:

"Loving me empowers you to obey my commands. And I will ask the Father and He will give you another Savior, the Holy Spirit of Truth, who will be to you a friend just like me—and He will never leave you. The world won't receive Him because they can't see Him or know Him. But you know Him intimately because He remains with you and will live inside you."

The Lord said He will speak to His people.

John 10:27 (King James Version) says:

"My sheep hear my voice, and I know them, and they follow me."

Let us as parents remember that there is no age limitation with God when speaking to His people. Our children are people; they belong to God, and He speaks to them.

The Voice of Truth—the Holy Spirit—speaks wisdom and truth into the hearts of our children.

This page intentionally left blank

The ABCs of a First Lady

About the Author

Dr. Barbara Layton is an inspiring and anointed teacher who empowers and encourages others to focus on the simplicity of the Word of God while challenging believers to apply God's Word to their daily lives. She faithfully serves alongside her husband, Dr. Rick Layton, as pastors of Refreshing Point Ministries in Shreveport, Louisiana.

Dr. Layton has earned a Bachelor's Degree in Biblical Studies, a Master's Degree in Biblical Counseling, and a Doctorate in Biblical Counseling from Friends International University in Merced, California. She is also a Licensed Pastoral Counselor with the National Christian Counselors Association.

Dr. Barbara Layton's mission is to motivate and inspire others to live life fully and joyfully while reminding them that they are the apple of God's eye.

Why I Worship

By Dr. Carla J. Debnam

Let's talk about the need for us all to find a time and place to worship God. Scripture tells us how we should worship, and that is to worship Him in spirit and in truth. We also know that worship looks different for everyone, and as pastors' wives we have not always felt the freedom to worship, especially at church. The spotlight on our way of experiencing the move of God and the presence of the Holy Spirit is subject to interpretation based on the thoughts of the congregation and sometimes even our husbands. This scrutiny has kept some of us in a box and bound by what others may say.

I appreciate my growth in this area. I was always concerned about the opinions of others, especially in church. It seemed like the place where I felt God and experienced breakthroughs was also the place I allowed to keep me in bondage. Being shy, introverted, and having a melancholy temperament all led to me being self-conscious about myself and whatever

I did. This included my worship, service, and praise to God. I felt like I was not free to be myself in church or other places for fear of being judged—unfortunately, sometimes by those closest to me. Whether this was what I imagined or not, it kept me from being free in the Spirit. As a result, I would leave my worship to private moments. It took years before I felt freedom from what others were saying and thinking about my expression of love for God. I don't believe that I am the only pastor's wife to feel this way.

This stronghold of fear, doubt, and being in the public eye was hindering me from accepting the freedom to flow and grow in my spiritual walk of faith. Attending retreats, conferences, and women's prayer groups were fertile ground and allowed me to mature and expand my definition of worship. As I yielded myself to the Savior, over time transformation took place. This progression from worshipping inwardly to worshipping unreservedly amazed me, as it might have others. Worshipping God was no longer only private, but also with others.

I believe as I freely expressed myself in the presence of others, my praise along with theirs became a sweet-smelling savor to the Lord. I learned that when I worship, I am transported to another place and receive the affirmation and acceptance of Jesus, which is most important and impactful for me. When we worship and give God the praise He is due, the words of the Apostle Paul come to life:

"But thanks be to God, who always leads us as captives in Christ's triumphal procession and uses us to spread the aroma of the knowledge of Him everywhere. For we are to God the pleasing aroma of Christ among those who are being saved and those who are perishing. To the one we are an aroma that brings death; to the other, an aroma that brings life. And who is equal to such a task?" —2 Corinthians 2:14–16 (NIV)

I was able to release my fears and invite God to fill me up to worship freely. This was not something I naturally was drawn to, but it grew into a desire as I learned more about myself and, more importantly, about what God has given me in return for my love and faithfulness.

I worship out of deliverance from low self-esteem, shame, and guilt that had built up over the years. I had a lot of baggage that kept me from worshipping God like He deserved. The pain of rejection and doubt overwhelmed me, and I felt hindered by the many weights I carried. I had to lay aside those weights like Hebrews 12:1 instructs us to do. I worship because I am accepted in the Beloved and am loved unconditionally and with an everlasting love. It took me years to embrace this, and therefore it was a roadblock to me experiencing God and freely worshipping in the power of the Spirit.

Knowing in my head that I was loved by God's one and only Son, Jesus, was not an immediate deliverance in my thoughts and actions. Overcoming the struggles of ministry, marriage, and motherhood was also something I had to face. My worship, as the song says, "is for real," and it came through many days of fighting myself.

Terry Crist, in the book Now You Can Stop Running, shares that *"sometimes you have to sing the hell out of your soul … and sing Heaven into your heart. Sometimes you have to sing your way into your right mind. Turning our focus from fear to faith transforms. Worship goes beyond the conventional forms of singing and prayer. It is an act of laying bare our fears, anxieties, and uncertainties before God."* This statement reminded me of why I worship. I worship for a breakthrough from the pain and hurts of my past. I worship to overcome my fears and the scars I developed going through childhood pain and dysfunction.

I know many of us have not had a perfect upbringing. Some of us were exposed to trauma and did not know it, and as a result made bad choices and have regrets about things that have happened to us and why they happened. But my encounters with Christians, church community, and ultimately Jesus Christ were the beginning of a fresh start for me.

My wounds are the foundation of my worship. They are my "why." On June 19, 2006, I preached my initial sermon from Isaiah 61:1–8. My theme was "Double for My Trouble" from verse 7: *"Instead of your shame you will receive a double portion, and instead of disgrace you will rejoice in your inheritance. And so, you will inherit a double portion in your land, and everlasting joy will be yours"* (NIV). This sermon was inspired by my quest to understand my life and ultimately my journey of faith. I was the poor, the brokenhearted, the captive, the prisoner, and the grieving. I was the one I was preaching to, and I recognized that I was not in this by myself. There were others like me waiting on God to come through. I wanted the shame I grew up experiencing to be swapped for a godly inheritance. I longed for justice to vindicate my hurts and to embrace the joy that God promised me. That joy was found in Jesus, and redemption from the heartbreak and disappointments was made possible through the sacrifice of Jesus and ultimately became the foundation of why I worship.

Until we encounter Jesus and release our wounds, worries, and the wrongdoings of others, our worship will be blocked, and we will miss our blessing. Worship has facilitated my path to wholeness. It has given me the strength to survive the worst of times and the energy to enjoy the best of times. Worship is what has helped heal me mentally, physically, and emotionally. Worship is a lifestyle that begins in the morning with praise, gratitude, and thanksgiving and ends in the evening with prayer, gratitude, and Scripture.

I end with this psalm of praise and worship. It is one of my favorite passages of Scripture and encapsulates why I worship:

"I love you, Lord, my strength. The Lord is my rock, my fortress, and my deliverer; my God is my rock, in whom I take refuge, my shield and the horn of my salvation, my stronghold. I called to the Lord, who is worthy of praise, and I have been saved from my enemies. The cords of death entangled me; the torrents of destruction overwhelmed me. The cords of the grave coiled around me; the snares of death confronted me. In my distress I called to the Lord; I cried to my God for help. From His temple He heard my voice; my cry came before Him, into His ears." —Psalm 18:1-6 (NIV)

This page intentionally left blank

About the Author

Dr. Carla J. Debnam serves as First Lady and an ordained minister at Morning Star Baptist Church in Gwynn Oak, Maryland. She holds a Master of Science in Pastoral Counseling from Loyola University and a Doctor of Ministry in Transformational Leadership from Ashland Theological Seminary.

Dr. Debnam is a Licensed Clinical Professional Counselor and the Executive Director of The Renaissance Center, where she works to promote healing and wholeness within individuals and communities. She also writes articles addressing mental health and spiritual wellness and frequently presents at churches and conferences.

Dr. Debnam stands firmly on the promise of Philippians 1:6, "Being confident of this, that He who began a good work in you will carry it on to completion until the day of Christ Jesus."

Xpectations

Lady Trudy Anderson

On August 7, 1994, we drove into the parking lot of New Jacob's Chapel Missionary Baptist Church in Clermont, Florida. I had childhood memories of driving past this church while heading to our headquarters church in Orlando, Florida, for our annual conventions.

I always thought this was our "other brethren's kind of church." Insider joke—laugh out loud. Well, little did I know that this Sunday would be the first of many. We served there nineteen years.

Xpectations

I was 24 years old.

In most people's eyes, I had been groomed for the role of a First Lady. My maternal grandmother and paternal grandmother were both First Ladies. Unfortunately, my paternal grandmother passed away when I was seven years old, so I did not have the opportunity to know her very long.

My maternal grandmother was also unable to spend much time with me growing up because serving as the First Lady of an African American Episcopal church meant relocating and serving a new congregation every few years. Because of this, I did not receive the A-B-C's and wisdom from her either.

Instead, I received my Xpectations of what was expected from my Aunt Florie Adams Hansberry.

In my opinion, Aunt Florie was the GOAT of First Ladies.

I spent every Saturday with her from the age of nine until I obtained my first job at Beall's Department Store in the summer of 1987.

My aunt taught me how to:

- Pack for church conventions
- Iron men's dress shirts and handkerchiefs
- Cook sweet potato pie, apple pie, lemon meringue pie
- Prepare collard greens, fried chicken, potato salad, macaroni and cheese

You name it—we cooked it.

She also owned and operated a store from her home. I learned how to count money backwards, without using a calculator.

I was afforded the opportunity to travel to annual conventions with her and my uncle, who served as the State Superintendent. My aunt served as the State Missionary and State Recording Secretary for the New Jerusalem Church of God, Inc.

It was Pentecostal—foot-stomping, hand-clapping, speaking-in-tongues, and dancing in the Holy Spirit.

A First Lady walked with her head held high. She wasn't arrogant, but she allowed the Holy Spirit to lead, guide, order, and direct her steps.

She was always cordial. She spoke to members of the congregation.

She did not sit in the back of the church. She found her seat, and rarely did she sit anywhere else once she settled in.

Sitting up front positioned you for spiritual warfare.

You covered your husband in prayer.

You prayed for the Holy Spirit to move throughout the service.

If someone needed help coming through, you were at the altar encouraging them while they called on Jesus. You labored with them until they came through, as we called it.

Xpectations and the Women of the Church

I was 24 years old.

I was young. I was the pastor's wife. I was the First Lady. I had no children yet. I observed them—and they observed me.

My gift made room for me.

I began ministering in song at the age of nine. Ms. Wendy Goins, our musician at the New Jerusalem Church of God in Dade City, Florida, heard something in my voice when I sang in the youth choir.

She was a disciplinarian.

We rehearsed seriously. She did not play the radio during rehearsal.

I still remember the three-part harmony she taught us. We stood—we did not sit during choir rehearsal.

We sang from our diaphragm.

- Sopranos—come with it.
- Altos—you better sing it.
- Tenors—you better roll with it.

In those early years at New Jacob's Chapel, I often sang before my husband preached.

He ministered at different churches, and I had the honor of introducing him. I never introduced him the same way twice. The Lord always gave me something different.

Even now, after all these years, the Holy Spirit still gives me a different direction when I stand to introduce him.

New Jacob's Chapel is also where I received my call to preach in December 2001.

My subject was "Get Off the Porch."

I will never forget it. Now my **Xpectations increased**.

Not only was I the First Lady—I was also a carrier of the Gospel of Jesus Christ.

My gift continued to make room for me.

When the opportunity presented itself, and with the permission of my pastor, I preached.

Xpectations in the Community

A First Lady never left home dressed any kind of way.

- No shorts
- No short skirts

By the time I entered the role, slacks were permitted—but they could not be tight.

There was no cleavage. Your blouse had to fit properly.

Your hair was done—no rollers, scarves, or bonnets. Those were for the comfort of your home.

You were representing:

- The Lord
- Your husband
- The congregation you served

Xpectations in the Workplace

It wasn't easy keeping it a secret that you were married to a pastor.

Once your colleagues found out, more was expected of you.

You had to move with integrity.

- No getting caught up in office gossip
- No invitations for drinks after work

Thankfully, I was never asked, so I never had to decline.

Xpectations Shift

We served at New Jacob's Chapel for nineteen years. Then we relocated to Fairmont, North Carolina, to serve at First Baptist Church, North Main Street, in November 2013, the fourth Sunday after Thanksgiving.

The Xpectations shifted.

The congregation was larger, and I did not have to serve in as many capacities.

I sought the Lord for direction.

The expectations were high. I was not an educator. I was not in a sorority. I was different from my predecessors. I was a preacher.

When I sought the Lord, the word I received was simple: **Love the people.**

There was concern that I would try to usurp authority and become a co-pastor. So I sat in the audience—not in the pulpit. I did not want anyone to get it twisted.

One of the first things the Lord led me to start was a book group. At the time I was still residing in Florida, so we held meetings by conference call. When I visited, we met in person at one of the ladies' homes. The groups grew. I was able to interact with the women, and we bonded. When you allow the Holy Spirit to lead you, you will not go wrong.

Once I moved to North Carolina permanently, we completed several books together and continued our book group meetings.

When Xpectations Become Heavy

What happens when you meet all the expectations, yet your dedication, sacrifice, and tireless efforts are no longer noticed or appreciated?

You keep showing up—even when life is life-ing. The joy you once had slowly begins to fade.

You continue to pray and intercede for others, even when you are struggling to pray for yourself.

You begin to wonder:

How could this be happening? This is not how the story is supposed to unfold.

"Lord, what am I going to do? Why are you allowing this to happen to me?"

You feel like you cannot talk to anyone. Even when God sends people to check on you, you cannot let them see the weight you are carrying. I was expected to be in the greatest season of my life.

Our son had graduated from college. He was navigating his career. He had rededicated his life to Christ.

Many times I wanted to call my spiritual mother and be transparent—but I couldn't. Another woman of God would text, "Just checking on you." And I would cringe, because I knew the Holy Spirit was speaking to her.

This pattern continued for several years.

Finally, on June 26, 2025, something shifted. At 5:05 PM, I walked out of the building, looked up at the most beautiful Carolina blue sky, and said: "Lord, it's in Your hands."

Healing

Over the next few months, healing began to take place:

- In my physical body
- In my mental health
- In my spirit

My joy began returning.

My posture of intercessory prayer returned.

My spiritual discernment grew stronger.

Yet even while experiencing this healing, I still felt invisible.

The Lord began opening doors of opportunity. When I shared the news, there was no celebration—only a passive nod or a simple "okay."

But I kept moving forward.

I made up my mind that I would no longer live in the chaos of thoughts telling me:

"You are no longer enough."

Instead, I chose to live for the Lord without reservation.

I began working on Trudy.

I spoke daily affirmations over myself.

My smile returned.

Final Word

My sister, do not allow the Xpectations of being a First Lady to cause you to lose who you are.

Walk with dignity.

And never allow your voice to be silenced.

You matter.

About the Author

Lady Trudy Hansberry-Anderson was born on January 25, 1970, to the late Celestine Hansberry and the late Ennis Hansberry, Jr. She was raised by the late Elder Edna Hansberry Stanback and the late Deacon Sam Stanback. She attended public schools in Dade City, Pasco County, Florida, and graduated with honors from Pasco High School in June 1988.

She was licensed to preach on December 29, 2001, at New Jacob's Chapel Missionary Baptist Church in Clermont, Florida, where she delivered her initial sermon. During her time there, she served in numerous roles, including Associate Minister, Leading Lady, Anointed Voices Gospel Choir Ministry Leader, Praise and Worship Ministry member, Women's and Youth Sunday School teacher, and Ministry Leader of the "From Weeping to Joy" Support Ministry, which supported individuals coping with the loss of loved ones and other life challenges.

She currently serves as the Leading Lady of First Baptist Church of Fairmont, North Carolina, where she ministers as a Praise and Worship team member, Mass Choir member, Sunday School teacher, and Women's Ministry participant.

Trudy earned an Associate of Arts Degree in Theology in 2009 from Life Christian University in Tampa, Florida, and a Bachelor of Science in Psychology in 2021 from Mid-America Christian University in Oklahoma City, Oklahoma. She is employed by the Robeson County Department of Social Services.

In February 2012, she founded CelEd D.I.V.A. Creations, a make-up artistry business named in honor of her late mothers, Celestine and Edna. She also serves as a Mary Kay Consultant.

Trudy and Pastor Rex Anderson will celebrate 36 years of marriage this year. She is the proud mother of two sons, Jarrett Travanthony and Joshua Nathaniel, and the step-grandmother of three.

Yes – For Your Consideration

By Lady Andrea McCargo

Words have always been sacred to me. My father is a poet and a songwriter, while my mother an educator, and both preachers and singers. Perhaps that's where my unwavering affection for language was born—at the point where rhythm, wisdom, and song intersect. As a lover of words, I sometimes forget just how powerful the smallest ones can be. Take yes, for example. Three simple letters, yet they carry the capacity to stretch us and reshape us in ways we never imagined. This compact word holds an undercurrent that draws us nearer to the heart of the Father.

When I accepted the invitation to be a part of this project and selected the letter Y, naturally, I was drawn to words like yes, yield, yoke, and yearn; each carrying layers of meaning tied to surrender, trust, and deep longing. To say yes is to yield, to lay down our own desires and embrace God's. It is to take on His yoke, trusting that His strength will carry what we cannot. Saying yes grafted me to the things God designed for me. Although I didn't know the plan, through divine intention, God yoked me to His purpose, strength, and soothing peace. The depth of God's love gently commanded a yes that I was oblivious to; however, it was expanding in the depths of my being from a young age. His mercy brought me to a place of surrender… a sacred exchange that compelled me to comply—not through fear, but through the solemn gift of compassion to accept me as I am.

More than two decades ago, prophetic words were spoken over my life—words that spoke of a journey marked by faith, obedience, and growth. Looking back now, I realize that the essence of that prophecy has been centered around this powerful word: yes. This word has been the genesis of a continuous unfolding, a sacred dance between divine calling and human response.

Paul's words in Philippians 1:6 resonate deeply within me: "I am convinced and confident of this very thing, that he who has begun a good work in you will continue to perfect and complete it until the day of Jesus Christ." AMP. Our yes to God is the spark that ignites this good work. It is an ongoing commitment that pushes us beyond who we were yesterday and opens the door to who God intends for us to become.

In the early stages of my walk with God and my growing desire for ministry, I remember praying, "Lord, I want You to use me." There was an uncompromising willingness in my heart to serve in a way that brought healing, freedom, and deliverance to others. I had witnessed men and women of God operate powerfully in their gifts, and I was deeply moved by how lives were transformed through their obedience. Witnessing this stirred a passion in me. I recall telling God, "You can trust me with Your gifts," because I truly wanted to be a vessel He could use. But looking back, I realize it started even earlier than that. Watching my parents walk out their faith left a lasting impression on me. Not only was I able to watch them, but they also allowed me to serve alongside them in the area of music. Their consistency, their prayers, and the way they loved people planted seeds in me before I even knew what ministry really meant. It wasn't about a platform; it was about surrender, about love, about being available. Even though I had a measure of spotlight, the spotlight wasn't my goal. I just wanted to see people free. That was and still is the heartbeat of my "yes." I want to carry the weight of God's presence in a way that would bring others into healing and wholeness, just like I'd seen growing up.

To say yes to God is not to step into ease and familiarity. It is, rather, to embrace the unknown and invite expansion. My yes to marriage to Bishop Joseph McCargo moved me from New York state to Maryland. Watching him operate so naturally in his calling, I convinced myself that it was enough for him to do the work while I just sustained the music ministry. I thought, "He's got it. I don't have to." But God never stopped tugging at my heart. Over time, I had to surrender my comfort and say yes to more. Saying yes meant stepping beyond what was familiar— beyond just singing, playing, or sharing the Word in safe spaces. It meant embracing a larger responsibility than simply being a pastor's wife. It was a weight I didn't want to carry at first. But as I've walked it out, I've discovered that my yes has been a pathway to freedom. It's allowed God to use me however He desires—without limits. In doing so, I've grown in courage, clarity, and confidence. My obedience has unlocked new levels of purpose I didn't even know I was carrying. Our yes pulls us out of stagnant places and propels us into movement—movement toward purpose, destiny, and divine transformation. It is a commitment to growth, even when the path is unclear and the outcome uncertain.

There is a divine reciprocity in our relationship with God: when we say yes, God also says yes to us. This strategically designed yes is an approval that instills confidence, affirming that we are seen, known, and believed in by the One who created us. God's yes emboldens us to believe in ourselves because He believes in us first. God's reciprocal yes goes to war for me, especially when my yes is being hit by waves of inadequacy and thoughts that I'm not enough. Let's be clear: saying yes to God doesn't exempt us from the fight. It invites it. We have to fight to keep our yes pure—a yes untainted by insecurity and definitely not buried under the weight of people's expectations that try to drown out His voice. His yes strengthens mine when mine feels shaky. His yes is not passive; it empowers, restores, and brings freedom. It opens doors of opportunity and, sometimes, closes others—guiding us with perfect wisdom.

Why is yes so pivotal? Because it stands at the crossroads between inertia and progress, between fear and faith, between limitation and possibility. When we say, "Yes, I will go," or "Yes, I will do," we are stepping into God's divine invitation to co-labor with Him. As evangelist and author Cherisse Stephens says, "All we need is one yes from God—permission to access His power and purpose."

My sister Dr. Grace Jones Spann, a wise and faithful voice in my life, often states, "I'm committed to my yes." Commitment to yes means stepping into God's plan, even when we don't have all the details. The reality is, when we respond to God's invitation with a yes, life often becomes unpredictable. Challenges arise, doubts creep in, and questions flood our minds: Did I hear God correctly? Should I have said yes at all?

My yes has tethered me to a divine purpose, a sacred power, and a peace that transcends understanding. It is a yoke that is not always burdensome but light—shared with the One who strengthens me. Each yes is a seed planted in faith, reliable to bear fruit in God's perfect timing. God knows how and when to prune us to produce more. Psalms 1:3: "And he shall be like a tree planted by the rivers of water, That bringeth forth his fruit in his season; His leaf also shall not wither; And whatsoever he doeth shall prosper."

Saying yes is not a one-time event but a daily posture—a yielding of our will to His, a continual invitation to walk in obedience. It is through this ongoing journey that allows God to perfect His work in us, refining our character, expanding our faith, and deepening our relationship with Him. Choosing the daily posture of humility brings exaltation. He promised it (1 Peter 5:6).

As I reflect on my journey, I am reminded that the more I lean into my yes, the more God expands my horizons. It is an open door to the adventure God has planned for me—a sacred trust that requires faith and perseverance.

So, I urge you to submit to the power of your yes. Yield to the cornerstone of your faith and surrender. Let it be the yoke that guides you to the unfolding work of God in your life. Remember that your yes is the turnkey that unlocks God's promises and accelerates you into all that He has prepared for you.

Say yes even if you have tears in your eyes. Say yes even if it doesn't make sense. Say yes confidently, knowing that God, who began a good work in you, is faithful to complete it. Your yes is more than a word—it is a covenant with eternity.

240

About the Author

Lady Andrea McCargo is the devoted wife of Bishop Joseph A. McCargo, Visionary and Senior Pastor of City of Hope International Worship Centre. Together, they have served in ministry for more than thirty years, both across the United States and internationally.

An ordained Elder, Andrea has a deep passion for holistic ministry, particularly in serving women, children, and couples. She ministers through prayer, healing, wisdom, and prophetic insight, offering retreats, leadership workshops, and mentoring opportunities for women in ministry.

A gifted worship leader and accomplished musician, Andrea's vocal and artistic excellence has been featured on national recordings and stages. She has worked with Charisma (Savoy Records), Mattie Moss Clark, Stephen Hurd, and others.

At City of Hope International Worship Centre, she oversees the Music, Worship, and Arts Ministry and remains actively involved in community outreach, prison ministry, and homeless care.

A proud mother and grandmother, Andrea is also the owner of First Lady's Salon in Glen Burnie, Maryland, where she has styled clients for professional photo shoots, including celebrity appearances.

Zeal While You Heal

By Dr. Malonia Hawkins

Healing is not a sign of weakness! Still being able to "Zeal While You Heal" is holy work. It's the process where God gathers up the shattered pieces of your heart and carefully begins to restore what was lost. Yet, if we're honest, healing isn't easy. It's the space between who you were and who you're becoming—a place filled with questions, quiet tears, and sometimes silence. I call it the place in the middle. It's a season where your faith gets tested, where you learn to trust God's heart even when you can't trace His hand.

Too often, when life breaks us, we stop moving. We wait until we "feel better" before we start living again. But healing doesn't mean halting. God never told us to stop; He told us to trust Him as we walk. He reminds us in Luke 17:14, "…as they went, they were healed." Zeal while you heal means keeping your fire alive, even when you're still tender from the pain. It's choosing to believe that God is still working behind the scenes—shaping you, strengthening you, and preparing you for what's next.

Pain, as cruel as it feels, always carries purpose. It doesn't come to destroy you, but to develop something within you. Every tear you've cried has watered seeds of wisdom. Every disappointment has shaped your discernment. There's a purpose even in the pain that you don't understand yet. Romans 8:28 reminds us that "all things work together for good to them that love God." Not some things—all things.

In 2009, I suffered the unexpected loss of my father. It crushed everything within me. For months I couldn't eat, sleep, or even pray. I felt like my laughter disappeared, and every day felt like survival. I grieved internally for so long that it began to shut down my body, and one day I woke up paralyzed from the waist down. Intermittently for four months, I was dependent on my husband and children for my daily care. I was broken and confused.

One day, after three years, I finally questioned God: "Why now? Why me?" I didn't receive an answer, but I received a statement that simply whispered, "Trust Me." I didn't understand it at first, but I obeyed. Slowly, God began to reveal to me that what could have been a tragedy was being replaced with peace. He reminded me that some only dreamed of what I actually had the privilege of experiencing. He showed me that, yes, I lost a parent, but I still had another one left. The more He showed me through the months and then the years, the more I healed. My heart began to mend in the very places I poured myself out.

That's the mystery of God—sometimes He heals you as you help others. My pain became my platform. What once broke me became the thing God used to bless others. That's the beauty of God's process. He takes ashes and turns them into beauty. He takes pain and transforms it into purpose. So don't despise your season of healing. It may feel slow, but it's sacred. It's where God is rebuilding you from the inside out. But while you heal, don't lose your fire.

Zeal is that divine spark—your passion, your drive, your "why." It's what keeps you pressing forward when everything in you wants to quit. The enemy would love nothing more than for your pain to put out your flame.

But that's when you must praise through the pain, worship through the weariness, and serve even when it's hard. Some of your most powerful moments will come from praising God while your heart is still breaking. Because it's easy to worship when life feels good—but real faith worships in the dark. Every time you lift your hands in surrender, even with tears falling, you're telling God, "I still trust You."

The Bible tells us in Galatians 6:9, "Let us not be weary in well doing: for in due season we shall reap, if we faint not." Healing requires endurance. Keep showing up for yourself. Keep showing up for your purpose. You don't have to have it all together—you just have to keep moving forward.

As God heals you, protect your space. Everyone can't go with you into your new season. Some people are connected to your pain, not your progress. They're comfortable with your broken version because it makes them feel needed or superior. But you've outgrown that. Healing means learning to say "no" without guilt and "yes" to peace. It means guarding your heart and not explaining your boundaries to those who benefited from your lack of them. Proverbs 4:23 reminds us, "Above all else, guard your heart, for everything you do flows from it."

You can't heal in the same atmosphere that broke you. You can't recover in an environment filled with doubt, gossip, or negativity. Your healing space must be sacred—a place of prayer, stillness, and truth. In that space, let God speak. Sometimes His silence isn't absence; it's strategy. He's teaching you to hear Him in new ways—through peace, through small signs, through stillness. The deeper your healing goes, the quieter your life may become. That's because peace becomes your priority.

As you heal, your perspective will shift. You'll start to see things differently—not through the lens of pain, but through the lens of purpose. Healing isn't only about feeling better; it's about seeing better. You begin to realize that what was taken wasn't meant to destroy you, but to reveal something deeper within you. The truth is, your scars don't make you less valuable—they make you more powerful. Scars tell the story of survival. They're proof that you made it. They're reminders that the enemy tried but failed. So stop hiding your scars. Instead, let them testify.

Learn to speak life over yourself:

"I am healing, but I'm still chosen."

"I am growing through what tried to break me."

"I am not what happened to me—I'm what God is producing in me."

Faith gives you the courage to believe in beauty while you're still standing in brokenness. It's trusting that even when life feels out of control, God is still in charge.

In the Bible, there's a woman who perfectly represents zeal while you heal—the woman with the issue of blood (Mark 5:25–34). She had been suffering for twelve long years, weakened and weary. People had given up on her, and maybe she even gave up on herself. But when she heard that Jesus was passing by, something in her reignited. She found a spark of zeal deep inside her broken body and said, "If I can just touch the hem of His garment, I will be made whole." She pressed through the crowd, through her fear, through her pain—and the moment she reached out, her healing came.

It wasn't just her touch that changed her; it was her zeal—her determination to keep reaching even when she was tired. That same fire lives in you. You won't always feel strong, but that doesn't mean your faith isn't still alive. Keep pressing. Keep reaching. Keep believing that your healing is closer than it feels.

Philippians 1:6 declares, "He who began a good work in you will carry it on to completion." God doesn't start something that He won't finish. You'll realize that the nights you thought would break you were the nights that built you. You'll see that the heartbreak that humbled you also positioned you for your breakthrough. What once felt like punishment was actually preparation. You'll laugh again—not because everything is perfect, but because you've made peace with your past and found purpose in your pain. You'll carry a different kind of strength—quiet, unshakable, and graceful. You'll know what it means to walk in wholeness—not because life is free of scars, but because you've learned how to live beautifully with them.

Healing isn't about returning to who you were; it's about becoming who God always meant you to be. So if you're still healing, don't lose your zeal. Keep your light burning. Keep your heart open. You can be healing and still called. You can be mending and still chosen. You can cry one day and lead the next—because God uses both your tears and your testimony.

You are not broken; you are becoming. You are not behind; you are being refined. Again, healing doesn't mean you're weak—it means you're brave enough to face what hurt you and trust God with it. Every scar tells a story, and every story has power. So let your healing shine. Let your fire burn. Let your faith speak louder than your fear. Because even now, in your healing, God is still writing something beautiful through you.

"Those who sow in tears will reap with songs of joy." —Psalm 126:5

You may be sowing in tears now, but your harvest of joy is coming. Keep your zeal while you heal—because you're still in the middle, and the middle is NOT the end!

About the Author

Dr. MaLonia Hawkins, a native of Annapolis, Maryland, is married to Apostle Donald Hawkins. Together they share five children, two grandchildren, and more than two decades of ministry experience.

Dr. Hawkins earned her Doctorate in Divinity from Harvest Time International Christian University and was affirmed as an Apostle in 2021. She is a Certified Advanced Life Coach, Registered Nurse, and the founder of Hawkins Haven Assisted Living Facility and Coaching & Consulting, where she promotes holistic wellness and healthy relationships.

Dr. Hawkins also serves as First Lady and Co-Pastor of Mimshach Empowerment Center in Maryland and Texas. Her life and ministry are dedicated to empowering others spiritually, physically, and financially.

Conclusion

by Pastor Jacqueline Renee Duncan

As we come to the end of this journey through the ABC's, may you be reminded that being a First Lady is not about perfection—it is about purpose. It is about walking with grace even when the road is heavy, loving deeply even when it is hard, and showing up fully even when you feel unseen.

Each letter in this book has been a reflection of the layers that make you who you are: anointed, bold, compassionate, devoted—and so much more. You are more than a title. You are a woman called by God for such a time as this.

Let this book serve as both a mirror and a mantle—a mirror to reflect on how far you have come and a mantle to carry forward the strength, wisdom, and joy of your calling. The role of a First Lady may not come with a manual, but it comes with a mission—and you, dear sister, are equipped for it.

Keep loving. Keep leading. Keep shining.

The world may call you "First Lady," but heaven calls you *faithful*.

Closing Prayer

Dear Lord,

Thank You for the call You have placed on my life—not just to stand beside my husband, but to stand firm in You. Strengthen me in moments of weariness, anchor me in seasons of transition, and remind me that Your grace is sufficient for every challenge I face. Let my words bring life, my presence bring peace, and my heart remain pure before You.

Help me to lead with love, serve with joy, and walk in wisdom. May everything I do bring glory to Your name.

In Jesus' name, Amen.

Affirmation

I am called. I am chosen. I am covered. I lead with grace, I love with purpose, and I live with joy. No matter what I face, I am never alone.

God has equipped me for every assignment, and I walk in His favor daily.

I am not just a First Lady—I am a daughter of the King.

Reflection

Take a moment to reflect on your personal journey.

- What letter or chapter spoke most deeply to your current season?
- In what areas do you feel God is stretching or strengthening you as a First Lady?
- Write a personal letter to your future self—a reminder of who you are, how far you have come, and what God has promised.

Remember: Your story is still being written—and it is beautiful.

About Leading Ladies of Integrity

Leading Ladies of Integrity, Inc. (LLOI) is a global network created to support and strengthen women serving in ministry leadership. Founded by Pastor Jacqueline Duncan, LLOI provides encouragement, resources, training, and connection for First Ladies leading alongside their husbands in ministry.

LLOI brings together Pastor's Wives: Leading Ladies of Senior Pastors, and widowed, separated, or divorced Pastor's Wives from churches around the world. Through workshops, fellowship events, and opportunities to connect in-person and through virtual platforms, LLOI creates a safe space where women in ministry can learn, grow, and support one another.

Motto: No First Lady Left Behind!

Mission: We are on a mission to bring together women from around the world, from every walk of life, to provide resources, support, education, empowerment, encouragement, and connection. We are a safe haven for all women.

Vision: To be a renowned provider of resource information, education, and empowerment to individuals seeking healing, restoration, and redemption.

Partner With Us

- We invite Pastor's Wives to become official partners with LLOI and enjoy a sisterhood filled with love, encouragement, and support. Visit leadingladiesofintegrity.org to partner.

Support the Vision

- You can also support LLOI by donating to help advance this support system for Pastor's Wives. Leading Ladies of Integrity is a 501(c)(3) nonprofit organization, and all donations are tax-deductible.

Contact Us

Email: infoleadingladies7@gmail.com

Tel: 301-221-2142

Learn more, connect, partner, or give at **leadingladiesofintegrity.org** as we continue advancing the vision of LLOI worldwide.

www.ingramcontent.com/pod-product-compliance
Lightning Source LLC
Chambersburg PA
CBHW051242050726
47594CB00001B/271